Praise for *Building Engaged Team Performance*

"We recognize our people are our greatest asset. With Engaged Team Performance, we were able to leverage the talent already in place without the distracting fanfare of the usual big change initiatives. The result: quiet delivery of improved and sustained performance."

—Amy Friedrich, Vice President-Specialty
Benefits Division, Principal Financial Group

"Using the principles of *Building Engaged Team Performance*, we were able to find common ground, commit to change, and design an enterprise technology platform that offers our agents unprecedented access to critical data, continuing to foster the team collaboration that has made us an industry leader."

—Jim Gelder, CEO, NFP Insurance Services, Inc.

"Building Engaged Team Performance leverages the key process concepts from Lean, Six Sigma, and Business Process Management (BPM), and takes them to the next level by integrating leading-edge human performance and teamwork methods. For many companies on a process excellence journey, *Building Engaged Team Performance* contains the vital missing ingredients that can enable teams to achieve significantly improved results."

—Rowland Hayler, former Vice President-Six Sigma, American
Express, and lead author of *Six Sigma for Financial Services*

BUILDING ENGAGED TEAM PERFORMANCE

ALIGN YOUR PROCESSES AND
PEOPLE TO ACHIEVE GAME-CHANGING
BUSINESS RESULTS

DODD STARBIRD

AND

ROLAND CAVANAGH

New York   Chicago   San Francisco   Lisbon   London
Madrid   Mexico City   Milan   New Delhi   San Juan   Seoul
Singapore   Sydney   Toronto

The *McGraw·Hill* Companies

Copyright © 2011 by Implementation Partners LLC. All rights reserved. Printed in the United States of America. Except as permitted under the United States Copyright Act of 1976, no part of this publication may be reproduced or distributed in any form or by any means, or stored in a database or retrieval system, without the prior written permission of the publisher.

1 2 3 4 5 6 7 8 9 0   DOC/DOC   1 5 4 3 2 1 0

ISBN   978-0-07-174226-9
MHID   0-07-174226-3

Library of Congress Cataloging-in-Publication Data

Starbird, Dodd.
    Building engaged team performance: align your processes and people to achieve game-changing business results/by Dodd Starbird and Roland Cavanagh.
        p.   cm.
    Includes bibliographical references.
    ISBN 978-0-07-174226-9 (alk. paper)
    1. Teams in the workplace—Management.   2. Quality control—Management.
I. Cavanagh, Roland R.   II. Title.
    HD66.S72 2011
    658.4'022—dc22   2010025357

McGraw-Hill books are available at special quantity discounts to use as premiums and sales promotions or for use in corporate training programs. To contact a representative, please e-mail us at bulksales@mcgraw-hill.com.

This book is printed on acid-free paper.

We owe so much to so many people, but this book had to be dedicated first to the team that piloted the concept of Engaged Team Performance, the Group Proposal Services team:

Tammy Auderer

Deb Blackman

Don Catus

Rebecca Cornish

Amy Duffy

Debbie Eller

Karsten Gebert

Katie Lippold

Alix Rogers

Julie Stanley

Trisha Streyffeler

Kenzie Theulen

Amy Ware

Craig West

Though we are the ones telling it, this is really *their* story . . .

Contents

Acknowledgments

W E HAVE MANY people to thank for their contributions to this book and for the things we have learned from them on our journey. We would like to recognize:

- Celeste, James, Aspen, Autumn, and Jade Starbird for their patience and loving support
- Jan and Barrett Cavanagh for enduring long periods of a closed door
- Deb Blackman, Amy Friedrich, and the rest of the strategy and process Center of Excellence team for their hard work and partnership
- Karsten Gebert for his visionary leadership and drive to push the envelope of change
- Ord Elliott for his vision, guidance, and friendship
- Cameron Karr for her partnership to deliver great solutions to our mutual customers and for her substantial help in gathering implementation examples and "Voice of the Reader" input

+ Kelly Babij, Tony Cann, Rosalie Escamilla, Jeanie Gabrielle, Deirdre Gengenbach, Evans Kerrigan, Teri Montz, Patrick Reilly, Beth Rothwell, Mark Welch, and the other team members at Implementation Partners, LLC, for their friendship and work ethic

+ Keith Lawrence for sharing his extensive Procter & Gamble experience with us

+ Knox Huston and the folks at McGraw-Hill for another great, professional publishing experience

And all the other people in all the stories in the book: we have enjoyed every step of the way in our journey with you to achieve *Engaged Team Performance.*

Prologue: The GPS Story

IT ALL STARTED on the back of a napkin.

In 2006, a business leader in the Specialty Benefits Division of the Principal Financial Group®, a large financial services firm, invited me to meet for lunch with a newly hired internal change agent. The business leader, Deb Blackman, was the director of Group Proposal Services (GPS), a sales support team that did quoting and proposals in support of the company's field distribution offices. I had been consulting for her company for a few years, teaching the typical Lean and Six Sigma process improvement tools and facilitating a couple of larger projects. And the change agent had just joined the company in a strategy director role, coming with strong process improvement credentials from General Electric (GE).

"Karsten Gebert, meet Dodd Starbird," she said. It was a key moment for all three of us.

The business leader had originally called the meeting to promote her strong vision for the organization learning to "manage with data" differently, and she pledged a willingness to experiment on her own team. She had been trying to get some traction for this idea for a while, and she was hoping that the strategy leader could drive the transformation and that our consulting company could help facilitate it. The strategy leader said that all he needed was a way to pay for the first project. So we did the typical "back of the napkin" sale on the table between our plates of Basil's pasta in the crowded restaurant:

"Tell me again, where do you think the opportunity is in your department?" I asked.

"We need better performance measures for efficiency," Deb explained. "I think our team is well led and motivated, and we have good processes, but we don't know how good we are. If we can measure this department well, then we can replicate that with less-efficient teams . . ."

"OK, just give me an idea of the kind of work you do . . . it's mostly quoting for sales proposals, right? So how many quotes does your team do per day?"

"Yes, we have a few peripheral things, but 95 percent of our work is quoting. Basically, we get a quote request by e-mail from the field office and create a proposal in the system. We do about 300 per day," she replied. I wrote "300" on the napkin.

Yes, there really was a napkin. We really wish we had kept it.

I continued, "So, give me an idea of how much work a quote takes; how much work time would you say it takes just to do one?"

This time she answered proudly, "We just did a time study on that—it's an average of 30 minutes for the main quoting work, maybe up to 35 including everyone who touches it." I wrote "300 units/day × 0.5 hour/unit = 150 hours/day" on the napkin.

Finally, I asked, "Tell me again, how many people did you say are in the department?"

Seeing the napkin and sensing now that there may have been a greater opportunity than she had originally thought, she replied, "There are 65. But 11 of those 65 are temps."

"Thanks for telling us all of that. And I know it's a little scary to let us play with your real numbers here. But remind me, have I ever told you about the *magic equation* for a transactional process like yours . . . ?"

The two of us had known each other for a long time, and so the conversation was more candid than many similar ones turn out to be. She knew immediately where the conversation was headed after she looked down at the napkin.

$$\text{Conceptually: } work\ time \times volume = people$$
(but in reality, it never does!)

So of course, 150 hours work time per day should take only 30 people working 5 hours a day, which is a good fully loaded assumption for a day's work that includes vacation, personal time off, meetings, etc. Even with the typical "overhead" of supervisors, trainers, and quality inspectors (which turned out to be 8 people), they were overstaffed.

The business leader, to her great credit, quickly accepted the high-level assessment as a real opportunity rather than an indictment of her leadership team. She knew the effort might expose her team to scrutiny in the short term, but she trusted that the results would make the team look good in the long term. (And sure enough, two years later, the GPS workplace was the most toured and benchmarked area in the division.)

I reassured her that this kind of opportunity really is typical for many businesses and departments that we initially assess, and it was fortunately all too believable for the strategy leader, who said, "Don't worry; it feels like a project here will quickly pay for itself. If it doesn't, I'll cover it somehow from my own budget. I'll make that commitment. When can you get started?"

A week later the project kicked off. Two years later, that process produced similar volumes with a team of only 38 people (including support and leaders). Cycle time had been reduced from two or three days (sometimes more) to 24-hour processing; customer satisfaction in field distribution had dramatically increased. Labor savings for the 27 people displaced to other roles was worth about $1.2 million per year, a 41 percent improvement in efficiency. *Most important, process changes initially drove a 17 percent efficiency improvement, but Engaged Team Performance (ETP) was the key to the other 24 percent that was gained.* ETP took the process and performance to the next level.

We initially used a well-known approach called "Lean Six Sigma Process Streamlining" to study and improve the process. And while the team did find some process design issues that were adding non-value-added work to the effort, we attained even more substantial gains simply by getting five hours of customer-valued work out of each person every day. In a later chapter we'll discuss Lean and Six Sigma, as well as a number of other useful process and organizational design approaches, but we have a few more-strategic questions to ask right now:

+ Why did a seemingly well-run department have such a great, and potentially obvious, opportunity to improve its performance?

+ Why did the business leaders in the area initially fail to see the opportunity?

+ Why were the people in the department only contributing 2.5-hour days of customer-valued work? Why didn't they just work harder?

+ Do similar opportunities exist to improve performance in other organizations, or was this example unusual for some reason?

We'll hope to answer all these questions, and more, in this book.

We'll start with the last question first because we want to make sure that everyone understands that the GPS department was not at all unusual.

In our travels to deliver consulting services for many different kinds of businesses, we have found that these kinds of performance opportunities are all too common. Over two decades, we've taken—and trained others to take—the Lean Six Sigma process-based approach for studying and implementing potential improvements, and we can prove that the approach has generally delivered strong results. We still believe strongly in it.

But we're also starting to see and hear too many stories of failed Six Sigma deployments and process improvements that evaporate when the financial impact is counted. The Six Sigma brand is no longer considered a magic bullet that works every time.

So while we still believe fervently in tools like Lean, Six Sigma, and Fluid Form organizational design, we have found that the process and organization are only parts of the equation. *Engaged Team Performance* also draws upon the other key part, the power of people; and while there has been equally great work done on the theories of engagement and self-managed teams too, there has been too little linkage between the process side and the people side. ETP is really a strong integration of both.

Regrettably, it seems that process and performance are quite disconnected at many companies. After a team studies and improves processes on the work floor in an operational area, leaders plan a new organizational design in a secret room somewhere in the HR department on the top floor, while mid-level leaders in another conference room conjure performance targets that are not at all related to the process team's newly discovered key drivers of process efficiency and effectiveness. Almost sounds like a conspiracy, doesn't it?

The truth is simpler and less malicious: human resources and operational process leaders just haven't integrated their disciplines very well yet. And even though their projects often succeed or fail based on change acceptance, process improvement and information technology practitioners have mostly focused on the "process and technical" aspects of the solution rather than on the people and organizational sides. Many of the problems we're asked to solve end up to be people- or performance-driven rather than simply being caused by process disconnects, especially now that some of the "low-hanging fruit" process issues have been fixed at many companies.

But let us be very clear about one thing: human resources (HR), continuous process improvement (CPI), and information technology (IT) practitioners are not to blame for this disconnect. It should be the role of *departmental leaders* to integrate their processes, their organizations, and the performance of their people in order to get optimum results. If you get out a napkin to do a little math and don't like your magic equation, you need to start by looking in the mirror.

This book will show departmental leaders how to use Engaged Team Performance to get the most out of their processes, organizations, and people. And of course, senior leaders, team managers, HR, CPI, and IT people may be interested as well. As you'll see, the concepts are fairly simple, but the journey is not easy.

Engaged Team Performance, What and Why

Engaged Team Performance at a Glance

If all you have is a hammer, everything looks like a nail.

Iᴛ'ѕ ɪᴍᴘᴏʀᴛᴀɴᴛ ᴛᴏ use the right tool for the job. This chapter will describe the key concepts of Engaged Team Performance (ETP), but we'll start by admitting that this tool set may not be for everybody. If you're a professional golfer, you may need to spend your valuable time reading other books instead of this one.

While a bit trite, the saying about the hammer and the nail is right on: sometimes people try to fit every problem into one tool set, and that doesn't always work out so well. Luckily, ETP is not just a hammer. It's a full set of performance improvement tools, shamelessly borrowed from the best thinking of the last 200 years, with concepts that have to be flexibly applied in different situations to drive optimum performance for teams. Most organizations can find great value in that kind of approach, but it's not for everyone.

Engaged Team Performance is the right approach for optimizing "production" teams—groups of people that share responsibility for delivering some kind of item to some kind of customer, whether in a manufacturing or a transactional or service environment. Production teams can create tangible products—say, manufacture a checkbook from a printing line or produce a can of beer from a packaging operation—but they can also produce softer yet just as critical deliverables such as process a claim, serve food at a restaurant, design a marketing campaign, or score points in a basketball game. When you think about it, teams produce almost everything. With such a wide definition, most groups of people in most organizations fall within this description, but there are certainly some "individual contributor" roles that don't fit the approach as well as others. You'll have to decide how well the description fits for your particular business or organization.

So while a professional golfer may not be the best team example, perhaps you remember the U.S. Olympic men's basketball team of 2004? The team of young NBA All-Stars probably had the 5 most talented players out of the 10 men out on the floor for almost every minute of each game that the team played in the tournament. Every team it played against was hopelessly outclassed. And there were some fantastic dunks, blocks, and other individual performances as Team USA lost to Puerto Rico, Lithuania, and Argentina on its run to the bronze medal. Ouch. Wikipedia's analysis:

> *Determined to put an end to these recent failures, USA Basketball has changed its philosophy and has looked to field complete teams instead of piecing together rosters of NBA All-Stars at the last minute . . . USA won gold . . . at the 2008 Summer Olympics with a dominant performance. (en.wikipedia.org/wiki/United_States_men's_national_basketball_team)*

Basketball teams may need ETP. Work teams at companies certainly need ETP, in manufacturing as well as service industries.

Hey, maybe even a golfer and her caddy count as a team too? *All* teams can benefit from Engaged Team Performance!

Engaged Team Performance is all about:

+ Capable processes with efficient flow

+ Focus to deliver consistently on critical customer requirements

+ Visual and available data for immediate decision making

+ The right staffing and resources for sustainable capacity

+ Deep personal skills and knowledge, supported by a long-term development plan

+ Standards and accountabilities for both team and individual performance

+ Team (not individual!) goals and incentives for team success

+ Fluid Form organization with norms to support collaboration and flexibility

+ Strong, yet engaging, leadership that lets the team own the execution

Integrated in a mutually supporting way, the above attributes help organizations to vastly improve their results, both in effectiveness of performance for customers and in efficiency in use of resources. The approach draws upon a core understanding of customers' needs and requires strong, proactive leadership.

Many readers may recognize core components of other methodologies in Figure 1-1; people who "grow up" under certain systems tend to put everything new that they learn into the context of the things that they already know, just like the saying about the hammer and the nail at the beginning of this chapter. So if you're looking at this and saying, "This is just [my favorite approach] done right," you're probably correct to some extent, but you'll see as we proceed that it's quite a bit more.

Figure 1-1   Engaged Team Performance Vision

Like many of the methods such as Lean Six Sigma that came before it, Engaged Team Performance is not all new. The approach draws heavily from other theories, methods, and tools. But it drives breakthrough gains in results that none of those prior methods can claim to have consistently attained. The secret is that ETP is a *combination* of great work from W. Edwards Deming's Total Quality Management movement, Motorola's Six Sigma, and Taiichi Ohno's Toyota Production System (the precursor to Lean Enterprise), with key ideas added from pioneers in employee engagement like Peter Drucker in *Managing in the Next Society,* Jack Stack in *The Great Game of Business*, and James Belasco and Ralph Stayer in *Flight of the Buffalo.*

In many ways, Peter Drucker predicted the advent of the ETP approach, emphasizing the critical role that "knowledge workers" would play in the future economy. While he envisioned many of the important differences and future trends, Drucker was more effective in strategically presenting the challenges in managing the work of the future than he was in tactically identifying specific solutions. Nevertheless, his work was foundational and inspirational for the consulting industry that he developed, and many of us owe more to him than we know.

But there are also newer theories that are key to the ETP approach, such as Ord Elliott's theory of Fluid Form organizational design. In his book *The Future Is Fluid Form*, Ord says that Fluid Form is about flexing to have "the right people in the right place at the right time." The book describes the value of reducing hierarchy and engaging employees at all levels to make decisions and move themselves to the point of optimum impact at the right time.

We would like to strongly acknowledge the influence that Ord's Fluid Form approach has had on our development of Engaged Team Performance; in fact, you can probably already sense that our ETP approach is really a tactical, focused adaptation of a Fluid Form business operating system designed specifically for departmental work teams. We'd certainly encourage our readers to read Ord's book as well.

As we proceed, we will briefly discuss the history of process and performance improvement. Engaged Team Performance powerfully combines great process improvement methods with strong teamwork and performance management concepts. While we will demonstrate that the recent widespread adoption of process improvement approaches has resulted in some outstanding breakthroughs in efficiency, the point of this book is that *current productivity gains are only the tip of the iceberg*. When process and performance improvement are combined, the results are more than doubled.

After illustrating some of the challenges in typical organizations, we'll demonstrate the steps to achieving Engaged Team Performance using the Group Proposal Services (GPS) example that we introduced in the Prologue, as well as highlighting some other stories from companies that have implemented the approach too.

The eight-step ETP deployment process is:

1. *Commit to change.* Find a burning platform for change.

2. *Measure and analyze the process.* Investigate the current process and customer requirements, and measure outcomes and work standards.

3. *Streamline the work.* Improve the flow of the process to deliver value efficiently.

4. *Make the work and data visible.* Make the new work processes, collaborative norms, and control measures visually obvious in the workplace.

5. *Organize the team.* Reorganize and right-size the team for the work.

6. *Set team goals.* Assess team performance and establish team goals.

7. *Lead the transition.* Make a rational plan, and develop the skills, tools, systems, and knowledge to move the team to the envisioned future state.

8. *Sustain Engaged Team Performance.* Demonstrate performance over time!

We'll conclude with guidance for senior leaders in how to enable (and not unintentionally *disable*!) the efforts of the engaged teams that work in their divisions.

In sum, Engaged Team Performance is about combining the concepts of a Lean Six Sigma *process* with the strong *team performance* of a Fluid Form organization, applying those principles down to the most critical level of a departmental working team, and sustaining that team to work efficiently and effectively for the customer and the business.

Does that sound simple enough? It's really not so hard, but few teams have done it well and then proved their ability to sustain it. We'll introduce you to some of those pioneering organizations as we go, and hopefully you can send us some new examples in the next few years as you implement ETP!

"As the Pendulum Swings"—A Brief History of Adventures in Business Improvement

W E'D LIKE TO take a quick look back at the more influential trends and programs that businesses have followed in the modern era. We're not going to go into a lot of detail; rather, we're hoping to give a sense of the key points of focus of each era, emphasizing the swings between production efficiency, quality, sociology, equipment, accounting, processes, and customer satisfaction. As shown in Figure 2-1, the pendulum of business improvement theory has swung widely and wildly, from precise management of dehumanizing small tasks to what some might call "touchie-feelie" attempts in social engineering; from efficiency to effectiveness; from process focus to customer centricity. Some eras built on what was learned in the previous years, while some apparently were simply reacting to the new conditions they encountered, but all conspired to deliver us here today.

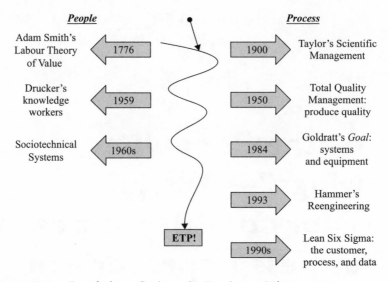

Figure 2-1　Pendulum Swings in Business Theory

Early Ideas

Many people think of Henry Ford as the inventor of the car. He wasn't. Ford's contribution was even more substantial: he figured out how to mass-produce cars cheaply and quickly, expanding the potential market by making them affordable and available for the vast majority of people. Ford was as much a philosopher as a businessman: his vision for the Model T wasn't just about making money; he wanted to introduce American families to the joy and the freedom of traveling.

So Ford revolutionized the landscape, both figuratively and literally, of the early twentieth century by taking a handcrafted car-manufacturing process and turning it into an assembly line. His original plant made 11 cars in its first month with the old process. A few years later, the same plant was making more than 1,000 cars each month. The new assembly process capitalized on the concept of the *division of labor*, breaking the car-making process into 84 areas that could be learned by different people.

By dividing the work into manageable chunks, each worker could be an expert in making one part of the car. The assembly line was born.

Ford didn't invent the concept of division of labor either. He applied ideas that had been around for decades, including thoughts from Adam Smith, a Scottish economist who had lived a century earlier. Smith saw both positive and negative potential impacts from the predecessors of the assembly line. From Wikipedia's entry on Adam Smith:

> *Smith believed that division of labor would cause a great increase in production. One example he used was the making of pins: One worker could probably make only twenty pins per day. However, if ten people divided up the eighteen steps required to make a pin, they could make a combined amount of 48,000 pins in one day. However, Smith's views on division of labor are not unambiguously positive, and are typically mischaracterized. Smith says of the division of labor:*

> *"In the progress of the division of labour, the employment of the far greater part of those who live by labour, that is, of the great body of the people, comes to be confined to a few very simple operations, frequently only one or two . . . The man whose whole life is spent in performing a few simple operations, of which the effects too are, perhaps, always the same, or very nearly the same, has no occasion to exert his understanding, or to exercise his invention in finding out expedients for removing difficulties which never occur. He naturally loses, therefore, the habit of such exertion, and generally becomes as stupid and ignorant as it is possible for a human creature to become . . . this is the state into which the labouring poor, that is, the great body of the people, must necessarily fall, unless government takes some pains to prevent it."*

Like Ford, Smith was a philosopher as well as an economist. Smith was worried that taking the division of labor too far would result in boring, mindless jobs that relegated the poor worker to remain downtrodden forever. Smith wasn't able to envision the vast technological advances that have shifted some of those repetitive roles to machines, so his fears did not fully come to fruition; but the disparity between rich and poor has continued to increase over time, and jobs have in fact become much more specialized as he foresaw.

As a philosophical aside, consider how that specialization of knowledge has driven our society to become more fragile now compared with Smith's time two centuries ago. Back then, families knew how to do most of the basic things to survive: grow food, make cloth, build a home, etc. Compare that to our more specialized skills now, and it's obvious that we're more productive as a whole but not as self-sufficient as individuals. The "Hurricane Katrina effect" of societal breakdown after a global natural disaster such as a devastating earthquake or another massive hurricane would actually be worse today than it would have been back then, since most people today would be forced to depend on others for help that might never come. The people of two centuries ago would have just picked up the pieces, rebuilt, and moved on. Unfortunately, as a planet we probably have that challenge coming someday, and it's just a matter of time.

While Henry Ford was designing his first production line, Frederick Winslow Taylor was pioneering the management consulting industry. As described in his book *The Principles of Scientific Management*, Taylor created four principles of Scientific Management for the study and control of human work:

1. Replace anecdotal work methods with processes based on a scientific study of the tasks.

2. Proactively select, train, and develop each employee rather than passively leaving the employees to train themselves.

3. Provide detailed instruction for and supervision of each worker in the performance of that worker's specific task.

4. Divide work between managers and workers, so that the managers apply Scientific Management principles to planning the work and the workers actually perform the tasks.

With the methods and driving influence of people like Taylor, people like Ford applied the concepts of Scientific Management to enable substantial breakthrough performance improvements from the division of labor. Today almost every process, from applying for a mortgage to going through the buffet line, is somehow modeled after Ford's Model T production line. As we'll see later, some organizations eventually took the assembly-line concept too far, though perhaps without all the evil consequences that Smith feared.

The Early and Mid-Twentieth Century

While Taylor was the father of the management consulting industry in the nineteenth century, Peter Drucker became its twentieth-century godfather. Drucker identified some of the key trends in the evolving economy, including the shift toward transactional processes. Today manufacturing is only about 30 percent of the gross domestic product in the United States, and the other 70 percent comes from the service sector. And regardless of whether manufacturing or service, the majority of job roles have transformed to become what Drucker called "knowledge workers" and are the opposite of the mindless roles that Adam Smith feared. The new worker has indispensable skills and knowledge.

Peter Drucker realized that the methods and approaches Taylor created to measure and manage manufacturing work had been thoughtlessly copied and misapplied to knowledge work, and in his book *Management: Tasks, Responsibilities,*

Practices, he lamented the lack of follow-through on Taylor's principles:

> *Frederick W. Taylor was the first man in recorded history who deemed work deserving of systematic observation and study. On Taylor's "scientific management" rests, above all, the tremendous surge of affluence in the last seventy-five years which has lifted the working masses in the developed countries well above any level recorded before, even for the well-to-do. Taylor, though the Isaac Newton (or perhaps the Archimedes) of the science of work, laid only first foundations, however. Not much has been added to them since—even though he has been dead all of sixty years.*

Under Drucker's guidance, management consulting took great strides in the later decades of the twentieth century. Visionary thought leaders like W. Edwards Deming and Joseph Juran led the Total Quality Management movement, while Taiichi Ohno applied the same principles with a slightly different focus in creating the Toyota Production System. But much of the effort was still oriented to improving manufacturing operations, and the transactional and service work again lagged behind.

Managers across the globe enjoyed reading *The Goal,* the book that Eliyahu Goldratt wrote as a fictional story to illustrate the impact of his Theory of Constraints (TOC) on reducing bottlenecks in an assembly line. As organizations became more complex to match their production lines, they applied Goldratt's ideas quite effectively to measure utilization of key *equipment,* while the concept of measuring the effectiveness and productivity of key *people* still failed to evolve at the same clip.

Sociotechnical Systems

Sociotechnical Systems (STS) is an approach that focuses on the role of the worker in the workplace in an attempt to find the optimum balance of excellence in technical performance and quality in people's work lives. Coined in the 1960s by Eric Trist and Fred Emery, who were working as consultants at the Tavistock Institute in London, Sociotechnical Systems provide much of the foundation of ETP, even though they were highly theoretical, cumbersome, and time consuming to implement and hence were not widely accepted.

The cornerstone principle of sociotechnical theory is *joint optimization*. In their book *Organizational Choice*, Trist and fellow authors Higgin, Murray, and Pollock explain: "Inherent in the Sociotechnical approach is the notion that the attainment of optimum conditions in any one dimension does not necessarily result in a set of conditions optimum for the system as a whole . . . The optimization of the whole tends to require a less than optimum state for each separate dimension."

Beginning with an organizational research article based on comparative studies of work crews in British coal mines, where, even as technology was improving, productivity was falling and, even with better pay and amenities, absenteeism was increasing, the theories were evolved into work designs based on the following principles:

+ *Responsible autonomy.* Shifting work to teams or groups with internal supervision and leadership, but avoiding the "silo thinking" by studying the whole system

+ *Adaptability, agility.* In an environment of increasing complexity, giving these groups responsibility for solving local problems

+ *Whole tasks.* Specifying the objective to be completed, with a minimum of regulation of how it is to be done

+ *Meaningfulness of tasks.* In the words of Trist et al.: "For each participant the task has total significance and dynamic closure"

Successful implementations of Sociotechnical Systems are relatively few and are either regarded as experiments or carefully shielded from view. Most are "greenfield" (built from the ground up) rather than improvements or transformations of existing plants, and all that we have discovered are based on a tangible product such as coal, coffee, gasoline, paper products, or dog food. Examples include:

+ *The flagship, Calico Mills, a weaving plant in India, 1953.* Comments Eric Miller: "Fifteen years later, the performance data for 1969-70 showed that the [Sociotechnical] groups were still consistently superior."

+ *Norway, 1962.* The Norwegian Industrial Democracy Projects demonstrated the positive impact of introducing Sociotechnical Systems arrangements in the workplace; however, expansion beyond the four field projects was difficult.

+ *Procter & Gamble, 1963.* P&G's first greenfield Sociotechnical Systems effort, which it called High-Performance Work Systems (HPWS), was a soap products plant in Augusta, Georgia.

+ *Mehoopany, Pennsylvania, 1966.* P&G constructed its largest-ever plant, using the new HPWS design to manufacture paper products like Pampers diapers and Charmin toilet tissue. After an initial learning curve, the team could produce and ship products to the docks of more traditional work system plants more cheaply than those plants could make them.

+ *General Foods, 1971.* Gaines Burgers pet food manufacturing plant in Topeka, Kansas.

+ *Other P&G sites, 1960s and 1970s.* Introduced into 21 plants in 6 countries processing all manner of consumer products.

+ *P&G, 1973.* Ord Elliott joins the team guiding the P&G Iowa City plant (toothpaste and mouthwash) on its journey to transform to HPWS.

+ *Shell Scotford Refinery in Alberta, Canada, 1984.* An oil-sands–fed refinery operated continuously as a Sociotechnical Systems design since its completion in 1984. With an objective to create a process-centered organization, in 2000 we had employees of a refinery in Louisiana benchmark with the Scotford teams. Although initially openly resistant to even the suggestion of learning something from a plant that uses a different feedstock, they returned awestruck and began their own transformation with gusto.

+ *Mid-1980s.* P&G began transitioning older plants to HPWS with varying degrees of success.

Significantly, the Procter & Gamble high-performance plants are on average 35 percent more productive than their traditional counterparts; and although P&G tends to "keep its lamp hidden" and not advertise its differentiators, the company is inundated with requests to benchmark or study the facilities and organizations. As a consequence, P&G is rightfully selective in allowing benchmarking voyages to its facilities.

William Pasmore writes that in spite of the successes, Sociotechnical Systems always faced "stiff resistance from those who preferred the comfort of traditional ways of managing" and "even some successful demonstration projects had shown signs of regression in the face of traditional authoritarianism." It takes a very real change in leadership style to give over control to teams of producers.

Another Successful Team Model—W. L. Gore

W. L. Gore created another notable divergence from the mainstream—a company founded in 1958 based on Teflon, with a focus on teams and communication. The company personnel have no ranks and no titles. Anyone can speak to anyone else, and the company is run as a collection of small "task forces" instead of traditional departments. Manufacturing plants have no more than 150 to 200 associates, so that the people all know each other; they can share or tap into knowledge and skills that wouldn't be accessible in a more conventional organization. Team leaders emerge rather than being selected. Unusually high associate satisfaction and retention are attributed to the unusual organizational structure and set of principles.

Kaizen, WorkOut, and Reengineering

Kaizen is a much misused word actually meaning "improvement" —not even "continuous improvement," as many people think. In Japan, the word is associated with typically small improvements discovered and implemented by the teams of producers who actually do the work. As practiced at Toyota for the last 50 years, the approach is equalizing or egalitarian in nature because people at all levels can participate in eliminating the waste and hard work of production. Roland's dad always said that "laziness is the mother of invention"—here it is in practice, the investment of effort as a team to make the hard work go away! More recently, Kaizen Events have sprouted up almost everywhere, convening gatherings of process stakeholders for a few hours or a few days to identify issues, offer suggestions, and then hammer out solution plans.

In the early 1990s, GE deployed a successful and popular collaborative problem-solving process, really just a more structured adaptation of Kaizen, called WorkOut. These action-oriented-team problem-solving sessions were ideal to bring cross-functional participants together to analyze and resolve simple process issues, and they began to drive great improvements in results for a diverse range of companies. In 1993, Michael Hammer then applied the same holistic process analysis concepts strategically in his book, *Reengineering the Corporation*. Beginning in 1994, Ord Elliott and

Implementation Partners refined GE's WorkOut with elements of Reengineering into the Action Forum Process.

The resulting methods, WorkOut, Kaizen, and Reengineering, had the same benefits—speed and action—and the same general weakness: sometimes they tempted people to jump from current state to future state based on process analysis but without appropriate data analysis, which often resulted in unintended consequences. The business improvement landscape was ripe for a more data-based approach.

Lean and Six Sigma

Consequently, two more major, and at the time competing, disciplines grew out of the melting pot of business-oriented thought in the 1980s and early 1990s. Like WorkOut and Reengineering, Lean and Six Sigma had process-based methods for problem solving built into their approaches, but they also began to use data in innovative ways to analyze processes before making decisions to change anything.

Lean Enterprise had strong roots from the Toyota Production System of the previous 40 years, and its name actually came from a book called *Lean Thinking* that James Womack and Daniel Jones wrote in 1996 as a sequel to their 1990 book about Toyota, *The Machine That Changed the World.* The Lean approach has probably contributed more than anything else to productivity improvement in the 15 years since.

Womack and Jones explain in *Lean Thinking* that the Lean approach "provides a way to specify value, line up value-creating actions in the best sequence, conduct these activities without interruption whenever someone requests them, and perform them more and more effectively. In short, lean thinking is *lean* because it provides a way to do more and more with less and less—less human effort, less equipment, less time, and less space—while coming closer and closer to providing customers with exactly what they want." Lean in its pure form as Womack and Jones described it in their books definitely has team engagement and human performance components, while most imitators seem to have focused mostly on the process theories rather than on leveraging the people aspects. Interestingly, the original Lean theories were quite effective in demonstrating a vision for a better process and organization, but the methodology was not quite so robust in explaining exactly how to make the right "leap" from current to future state.

Six Sigma began in 1987 at Motorola as a product design quality effort and was then transformed by General Electric into a more holistic business improvement system in the decade of the 1990s. It's hard to believe that it has been 10 years since our team wrote the bestselling book *The Six Sigma Way*, in 2000, to explain the wild success of GE's approach and popularize the Six Sigma brand name. The Six Sigma approach was really the first integration of quality, root cause, and process improvement principles to incorporate a "simple" five-step execution process, and the book became a cookbook for the thousands of people who were trained to lead the process improvement wave of the future.

The last decade has mostly seen enhancements to the two major approaches, most significantly the combination of Lean and Six Sigma (as well as other lesser-known competing methodologies) and the transformation of the methods to apply to transactional and service processes just as well as manufacturing. Lean Six Sigma techniques are still being taught and practiced across the world, generally to great positive acclaim and results.

Centering the Pendulum

And in all that flurry of business process improvement work, a couple of great ideas came along a little too soon and got trumped by the sexier brand names of Lean and Six Sigma. In 1992, Jack Stack wrote *The Great Game of Business* to explain the value of open-book management. His simple yet radical premise was that rather than telling employees only what they "need to know" to do their jobs, management should make the entire business transparent to the whole team. As the president and CEO of the Springfield Remanufacturing Corporation, Stack turned his company around by treating the success of the business as a game and sharing all the results—the numbers—with his entire team. Rather than keeping business performance a secret, he got engaged buy-in from his workforce by showing everyone the truth.

While Stack shared strategic performance information with his employees, James Belasco and Ralph Stayer followed in 1993 with a more tactical approach for engaging people in the business. Their book, *Flight of the Buffalo*, encouraged managers to think differently about their roles. Instead of engaging employees, managers sometimes unintentionally constrict their teams' ability to get work done. Their conclusion was that leaders need to be proactive instead of reactive:

> *I told my people to stop sending me all those reports and data, and instead list the decisions they thought they should be making and could make without consulting me. When the list wasn't long enough, I challenged them to rethink it. I started sending back memos unread and asked the data processing department to take my name off many distribution lists.*
>
> *My change disturbed some people at first. They had difficulty making the shift. With coaching, they finally got the message. Leadership isn't processing papers. It's about making things happen . . . The leader encourages people to take self-directed actions to achieve great performance and remove obstacles that stand in their path.*

These two books about employee engagement actually started the process improvement journey for Dodd. In 1997, a division vice president at Coors Brewing Company handed junior leaders in his organization copies of both books and asked us to apply the concepts. I had a hard time looking in the mirror the next day. I was one of those leaders who carried around a clipboard with a list of action items, busily writing down and prioritizing problems. Every time the members of my team encountered an issue, they were well trained to immediately report it to me instead of fixing it. I was enabling the problems instead of the solutions.

At the time, my job was to supervise a beer packaging line, and my team had encountered a productivity problem. Our production numbers had been consistently falling in the last few months, and we were right below the "volume goal" that the company had set for our manufacturing line. So I went into my next team meeting and surprised them: I showed the team the numbers on our recent performance, and I said, "I'm now going to leave the room for an hour, and when I come back, I'd like to see a list of causes of the issues, a list of solutions that you, the team, are going to implement, and a list of things you need from me." I walked out.

When I came back, their list was full, and mine was empty. They implemented solutions like "rotational coverage of equipment by senior specialists to check machine setups" that allowed the most experienced team members to visit each of the team's machines every day. Funny enough, if I had suggested that solution, I probably would have received a grievance form for breaking departmental seniority work practices; but because it was their own idea, nobody thought to challenge it. The numbers quickly jumped back up into the acceptable range, and I never had to fix anything there again. I just made sure the members of the team knew how we were doing, and I stayed out of their way.

We hope you've been able to hang in here for the history and philosophy lesson, because the past helps explain the gaps in the current state of the business and consulting thought process. In short, people have studied the technical side of work and process improvement for more than a hundred years, and we've glossed over equally important work about the psychology of the human worker. With knowledge workers now forming the majority of the economy, the combination of technical analysis methods with human teamwork and motivation approaches has been haphazard at best, and counterproductive at worst.

This book is all about forming the appropriate combination of the technical and human sides of work. As you'll see, each side holds a key part of the opportunity. Both sides are critical and have to be considered together.

Chapter Summary

Process improvement has a long history, with great businesspeople like Henry Ford and Taiichi Ohno applying theories from great thinkers like Adam Smith, Frederick Winslow Taylor, and Peter Drucker to generate breakthroughs in efficiency and quality.

+ Sociotechnical Systems exposed the opportunity for teams to dramatically improve performance, but most implementations were kept quiet by the companies leading the efforts.

+ Two significant and well-publicized process improvement methods, Lean Enterprise and Six Sigma, grew separately from the best process improvement concepts of the previous century. In the last two decades, these two approaches have been effectively combined and deployed by many companies across the world to improve process efficiency and effectiveness.

+ Performance improvement theories, while proved just as effective as process improvement for driving results for organizations, have not yet been integrated fully with the process improvement methods.

Engaged Team Performance combines both process and human performance improvement to deliver even better results than the two disciplines do individually.

3

From the Outside In: Understanding the Customer Experience

YOU MAY HAVE noticed a pattern in the histories given in the previous chapter—each one focused efforts on either the product and equipment, the work process ("systems"), or the organization's structure. Most companies have passed through one or more of these philosophies in their quests for greater competitiveness, and a few have gotten mired in one along the way. The more recent of these approaches have included some acknowledgment of the importance of the customer, perhaps most pronounced in Six Sigma where a substep of the Define phase of a project is to reach out and collect Voice of the Customer (VOC) and where company deployments are encouraged to include a VOC program.

Regardless of the methods used, a firm connection to the customer is essential for properly identifying and implementing just about any kind of improvement. As a component of process improvement methodologies, Voice of the Customer often became simply a one-time activity within each project. But today companies are creating formal, proactive programs to listen to the customer and act on the information they hear.

Voice of the Customer

In the last few years, greater emphasis has been placed on listening to VOC through surveys and trend analysis, initially highlighting product and process shortcomings, customer support team (help desk) performance, and health of the relationship. Gradually, recognition of the importance of understanding the overall customer experience has evolved from the discovery that a great product or service or an awesome sales team is probably not enough foundation for a long-term relationship. According to Jeff Zabin of the Aberdeen Group:

> *Never before has the voice of the customer been so loud. And never before have companies been so keen to not only pay close attention to customer opinion, positive or negative, but to carefully analyze customer feedback to generate actionable insights that improve customer experience quality, drive new product development, and ultimately, increase shareholder value. That means moving beyond ad hoc surveys and point solutions that focus on a single channel, product, line of business, geography and/or aspect of the customer experience. In an ideal world, it means implementing technologies, business processes, organizational resources and performance metrics that enable companies to capture, integrate, analyze and act upon customer feedback in a holistic fashion, across all customer touchpoints, all parts of the company, and all stages of the customer relationship lifecycle, on an ongoing basis.*

"In today's economic environment, focusing on customer satisfaction and loyalty is more important than ever," said Cameron Karr, vice president of marketing at MarketTools. "As a leading indicator of loyalty and retention, customer satisfaction impacts overall business performance and the bottom line."

In the last few years, a concept to measure net customer loyalty briefly became a huge fad and has since settled into being a good idea that fits well within other overall approaches. The strength of the "net" idea is that it can drive to a single measurement of overall customer loyalty called the "net score," which is basically a measurement of the difference between the percentage of customers who would highly recommend a company's products or services and the percentage of customers who wouldn't. Many companies have modified the approach to fit their own needs, but generally the idea has achieved widespread use as a way to measure overall loyalty and its impact on the health of the business. While other methods (including Lean Six Sigma and ETP) may have more robust techniques for analyzing survey data and coming up with detailed root cause analysis to drive *improvement* of the net loyalty score, customer loyalty programs are easy to launch and thus are driving greater focus and gathering critical information that together are contributing to a drive for greater performance effectiveness.

James Spicer, president of SimplexGrinnell, provides another excellent example:

> *We strive to exceed the expectations of our customers and provide the best possible customer experience. In order to meet our commitment to providing the best fire and life-safety services, products and solutions, we need to hear feedback from our customers. We need to know what we are doing well, so that we can deliver strong, consistent performance across our 150 local offices in North America. We also need honest input from customers about opportunities for improvement, so we can quickly address any issues or challenges.*

One of the first successes at SimplexGrinnell was improving the net customer advocacy score (percentage of advocates less the percentage of detractors) of a poorly rated region by 8 percent in 90 days. The company's approach required key personnel to participate in an analysis of the customer satisfaction data, including the review of individual comments; then the company developed and implemented changes to engage with and more proactively interact with customers. Simple solutions like confirming appointments each morning for that day and striving for a "first-time fix" were identified and implemented, while longer-term process and IT changes were prioritized to get further gains.

"This is an important model for driving improvements in customer experience and retention within those local offices demonstrating lower customer advocacy scores," says Karl Sharicz, manager of customer intelligence.

A Focus on the Customer's Experience

An equity fund firm that holds accounts from his mother's estate has become one of Roland's least favorite Web sites. First you identify yourself as an "Individual," next you select "I'd like to log in," and then you choose the type of shares owned from a list of cryptic codes ("How the heck do I know; I didn't buy them!"). Only then are you given the keys to the kingdom (an opportunity to log in). Surely not customer-friendly.

Peter Merholz, in *Subject to Change*, speaks of a metaphorical company, FinanceCo, as having silos that produce statements, deliver Web content, invest, and interact personally through account advisors. Each function had its responsibility and was executing it to the best of its ability. "We explained to FinanceCo that they needed to treat all these touchpoints as components in a coherent system. And, that system had to have two key objectives: 1) allow customers to accomplish their goals, by 2) moving the functionality to where it was most appropriate in the system. Our primary recommendation was to redesign across the touchpoints, with an eye to the customer's experience." Oh, how I wish FinanceCo were my mom's equity fund.

Peter's company, Adaptive Path, goes one step further, advising that customer research deliverables should be clear and engaging and tell a story. "One particularly effective way to make deliverables more engaging is through the use of *personas*, archetypes of your customer and users that can act as surrogates for those people in the design process." More thorough than stereotyping the ubiquitous "soccer mom," the company suggests creating a one-page "résumé," naming the users as individuals with pictures, behaviors, motivations, and real problems. "The best personas tell their story in their own words, often using quotes." Personas are powerful because they feel real, and they build a human connection; they capture the imagination of the organization, sharing insights and empathy. Can I volunteer to be the persona for that equity fund company?

We'll make a simple statement here, and then we'll follow it throughout this book: *engaged teams have to be focused on performing to meet customer expectations.* Processes, activities, measures, goals, and accountabilities that don't support or align with key customer needs are a waste of time and energy. Teams and team members need to care about the customer's needs and experience because customer loyalty is the only real source of long-term job security.

Chapter Summary

+ Most approaches for information technology deployments, process and organization changes, and performance improvements include some type of Voice of the Customer method to gain a focus on the customer's needs prior to designing a solution.

+ The customer's experience should provide the external target for any and every improvement or transformation of business performance.

+ A formal program for listening to the Voice of the Customer can allow a company to take the initiative in gathering critical information and making proactive decisions.

4

Individual Goals: What You Measure Is What You Get

I N THE HISTORY lesson in Chapter 2, we discussed the evolution of business management thinking, and obviously one of the key conclusions is that the body of knowledge has improved over time. Unfortunately, there is one prevalent myth from Taylor's Scientific Management that has survived unscathed in most companies today: the fallacy of the universal effectiveness of *individual goals.*

Individual goals don't always drive the intended performance, and they're often counterproductive. Not sure if you believe that yet? Read on!

*Individual goals are not quite the same thing as "performance standards" or "accountabilities"—we'll define the differences further in a later chapter.

Have you ever called a service provider, or perhaps a help desk, and then realized that the call center associates were being paid or punished for call duration? You know what we mean; that's the call center where:

1. Your first call is a hang-up and you have to redial (the associate just improved his average time since the first call took only one second).

2. When you finally get through, you get transferred a few times (each person gets to count that short time with you as a call).

3. You get rushed off the phone at the end when you had another question (once your representative has run out of time).

Call centers are the prime example of an operation with a computer system that allows management a false sense of security by tracking the call center associate's every move. Other new technologies such as global positioning satellite (GPS) transponders in delivery trucks have the same effect: they give great information to management about where employees are. Unfortunately, they don't tell anyone what they are doing or, more important, *what they should be doing*; if you measure and reward the wrong behaviors, you get more of them!

Individual goals aren't all bad, but they sometimes cause more problems than they solve. We'll tell you a few stories about that here, but we suspect that you've seen the negative effects personally as well. Here are a couple of our favorites . . .

Measuring Activity Drives More Activity

An insurance carrier implemented a workflow system for tracking applications through the policy issue process and managing the performance of its case managers and underwriters. The premise was that the company could account for and drive productivity by measuring all the subtasks—"touches"—that combine to produce the overall result of writing a new policy for an applicant. These cases require gathering and consolidating several (sometimes many) "requirements"—documents and bits of information that the underwriter will ultimately use to assign the applicant to a risk class. In the event that a document had not yet arrived as expected, the workflow system required that the case managers schedule follow-ups to either check the system to see if the document had been received or contact the broker or applicant to confirm that it was on its way.

At one meeting, early in the project, Roland led the team to construct a rough "sticky note" map of the process on the wall and began to flesh it out with volume and timing estimates.

"How often do you follow up on those missing requirements?" I asked.

"We have follow-ups scheduled at different intervals depending on the type of requirement," a team member responded. "Most of the activities are scheduled three to five days apart, depending on how long we expect the requirement to take to arrive."

"Do you have to follow up even if you suspect that the customer won't be ready to send the requirement yet?" I inquired. "I mean, sometimes it has to be different than three to five days, right?"

"Well, we have to follow up on the day it's scheduled in the system, since our goals are set based on the follow-ups being completed," was the reply. "Most of the follow-ups don't actually change the result in getting the requirement anyway. It comes when they're ready to send it."

"Hmmm . . . ," I murmured, thinking that there were some unnecessary touches here.

As we investigated the goals for the team members, we found that there wasn't a goal for the number of policies issued—that wouldn't have been "fair" to the case managers, since they are quite dependent on the applicants to return the needed requirements. Instead, the individual goals were based on numbers of activities (like the outgoing follow-up phone calls or e-mails) that the case managers did. That goal, of course, was fair to the team members, but it just resulted in more activities.

The case managers' behaviors had become consistent with the goals: they followed up on expected requirements relentlessly. "Ding!' Another transaction recorded, ever closer to my daily goal." The best could do more than 100 in a day. But those extra follow-ups were expensive and had only a marginal effect on the overall process timing.

The team eventually designed a "jet application" process that enabled applications that arrived with all the needed requirements to go to the top of the queue and get processed immediately, rewarding those applicants and brokers who turned in complete applications with faster service. Of course, sometimes the case managers still need to order and wait for an additional requirement, so they reset the follow-up frequency based on the impact that the follow-up is expected to have. Overall cycle times improved, and brokers cite the company as one of the best in new business service.

The positive side of aligning individuals' goals with their activities is that many things can be measured and reported; the negative side is that they are usually the "easy" or "available" metrics such as production and productivity numbers, counts of "things" produced, and time expended. If these goals are not clearly and carefully linked to a key business or customer need, the goals may drive more activity without driving a corresponding result.

Imbalanced measures will drive behaviors inconsistent with the customer and company goals. Activity measures, even if they're "fair" and available, will probably just drive more activity.

An executive from another company has a similar perspective: "Start with what you want to know, not from what you have," says Jane Stackpole, head of strategic planning and analysis at Silicon

Valley Bank. "Create data, make it whole, get information from it, and act on it." The more holistic measures may be more painful to collect, and they may be more applicable to a team than to an individual. But they will drive the right behaviors!

Perfect Installations

In 2008, we were asked to lead a project to help a client improve the installation process for a complex business-to-business product. The installation process was quite complicated, for both the company and its customers. After the prospective customer agreed to purchase the new product, the team had to gather and data-enter, into multiple computer systems with different purposes, a great deal of information about the customer's company.

For quite a while, our client's distribution (sales) team had been forwarding concerned comments about the installation process from customers and field sales team members, complaining about computer system problems and mistakes made by the home office installation team. Distribution leaders claimed that at least half of the products installed had some kind of problem with the installation, which sounded like a serious problem to almost everyone. While the system problems were known and some fixes for them were already in progress, the persistent reports of human errors were more perplexing.

When we interviewed leaders of the home office installation team, we found that they honestly weren't sure whether to believe the stories about the human errors. One person observed that he'd heard the same three horror stories from the field multiple times, and he was pretty sure that the vast majority of products were installed seamlessly. Of course, the seamless ones don't usually get much publicity, so we thought he might have a good point. The team didn't have a centralized complaint tracking system, so we quickly implemented that to help identify the extent of the impact.

While that data collection effort was getting under way, however, we decided to corroborate the evidence of the potentially overblown field complaints by looking at the home office team's internal quality assurance (QA) audit results. When we discussed the QA results with a team leader who monitored the program for the department, he explained that each team member had a goal of 95 percent but that the department was considering changing the goal since 94 percent seemed to be more reasonable for most people to consistently attain.

The audit process had been designed to provide *individual* performance feedback to all team members, so that every team member had a representative sample available for performance evaluations. Coincidentally, the department average for all team members was 95 percent. But that's not bad, right? In grade school, we learn that 95 percent is an "A" grade. And the field sales team seemed to be reporting a very different level of pain. As we heard this, the look on the department leader's face said, "I told you so."

But when we asked for the "percent of products installed perfectly" (without any errors at all), we were disappointed to find that the QA data were not able to provide that measurement since the QA reviewers weren't required to write down the identification numbers of the ones that they inspected. A department leader explained that the purpose of the data was only for measuring individual performance, so the QA reviewers weren't collecting or monitoring the overall result for each customer. Remembering the complex data entry process, we casually asked, "Remind us how many sequential steps there are in the installation process? How many of your people touch each case?" The answer: 10. We had our smoking gun.

When you flip a coin, there's a 50 percent chance of a head and a 50 percent chance of a tail. If you wanted to calculate the probability of getting a head twice in a row, you'd multiply 50 percent times 50 percent and get an answer of 25 percent. Interestingly, the chance of flipping 10 heads in a row is 0.50 to the 10th power, or only 0.1 percent (1 in a 1,000). Try it sometime!

Applied to business processes, this concept is called "rolled throughput yield." If there are 10 associates touching a case, and all of them are 95 percent good, the chance of getting a perfectly clean case through the whole team is 0.95 to the 10th power (0.95 × 0.95 × 0.95, etc. . . . 10 of those!), which equals only 60 percent. Add to that some system issues, and the data completely supported the allegations that were coming from the field distribution team.

Yes, a team of 10 data entry associates who are all touching the process with solid 95 percent "A" grades still delivers a 60 percent "F" for the customers! When we actually got the "perfect install" measurement calculated from real data, and including the other nonhuman-error causes of issues as well, the data confirmed the field team's initial conclusion: only 40 percent of products were installed perfectly. The individual measures and goals were providing a false sense of security and reinforcing a misperception of the level of performance that would be needed for the team to be successful.

As the project progressed, the leaders of the group took substantial initiative to change the mindset of their junior leaders and team members, de-emphasizing the individual performance and setting team goals for "perfect installation" for each customer. With some good work on the process and systems as well, the team made vast improvements to the results over the next few months; and aside from an occasional anomaly, the field has been quiet ever since. The department has more recently been working on a project to streamline the number of touches (handoffs from one team member to another) per installation, which will both vastly reduce work time and further improve the ability to do perfect installations.

The Myth and Reality of Individual Goals

The world is full of incentive plans, rewards, and variable compensation schemes that are based on the two premises that

(1) results are a function of effort, and (2) effort is a function of reward. Therefore, the more we pay for results, the better results we'll get, right? We have to admit that we believe this to a certain extent as well, so we'll be very careful in trying not to offend the salespeople and others out there who are paid on a variable basis for their performance.

But we'll flip the premise around, and we'll suggest that this revised statement is better: *when the results are a function of effort, effort is often substantially a function of self-worth, recognition, incentives, and rewards.* While recognizing the key concept that money is not the only motivator for people, the more important difference here is obviously that sometimes the results are a function of effort and sometimes they are not.

Stretch Goals

Let's play a little game: suppose a department decided to improve performance of a group of data entry specialists by giving them double pay if they could get their average data entry time per case of 30 minutes down to 10 minutes. Sounds like a better deal for both management and the employees, right? That's called a "stretch goal" because it asks employees to strive for greater performance than past experience has demonstrated is sustainable.

Is it even possible? Probably not. If the data entry task currently takes 30 minutes on average, and without dramatically changing the tools and process, even the fastest workers wouldn't be able to consistently shave 20 minutes off their average time. So the employees would see the stretch goal as an obvious ploy from management to try to get them to work harder, and the perceived impossibility of it might cause them to think their leadership is out of touch with their work and process. The employees would probably resist the goal.

But what would happen if the incentive were huge, like double pay? Perhaps some bad behaviors:

+ *Cherry picking.* Some data entry specialists would search the work queue for the easy tasks and take them from the middle of the pile.

+ *Shortcuts.* Some data entry specialists would find a way to meet the time goal, even if the work product would not be exactly perfect.

+ *Other creative ways to cheat.* We'll leave this to your imagination, but often this includes finding new ways to measure things, like breaking one task with three versions into three separate tasks in the system . . . triple credit!

Even worse, the honest, hardworking data entry specialists would fail to meet the goal, see the rewards being reaped by the cheaters, and then perhaps decide to leave the department or company.

We're not saying that incentives tied to individual goals don't work. As we saw in the insurance requirement-gathering example earlier in the chapter, we're saying that sometimes the incentives work just fine but still don't drive the intended result. People find a way to deliver the results that are measured, and we know that sometimes bad measures drive bad behaviors. Most of the time, the bad behaviors are not even really intentional. In the vast majority of organizations, people come to work with positive intent to do a good job and please their customers. Their goals often drive them to do things that they know are wrong, and they rationalize their behavior because they think that their management also knows the goals are imperfect.

So, let's now presume that we actually figure out the right measurements and then make individual goals to support them. That will work, right? Not exactly.

The other problem with individual goals is that they only work when the goal is *within the range of sustainable effort*. As we already demonstrated with the example of the potential 10-minute data entry task, an impossible goal doesn't motivate anyone, because people know it's impossible. A stretch goal may get people to sprint for a while, but eventually they'll burn out and stop caring. Even the prospect of time-and-a-half overtime pay eventually wears thin when people get tired. Most people want the opportunity for some overtime, but hardly anyone likes mandatory overtime every day.

Stretch goals are more effective when the need to stretch is short term, the team perceives that sprinting will accomplish the goal, and the rewards are team oriented. The members of a team will often come together to meet a short-term volume influx, survive a system outage, or work through a snowstorm if they see a greater purpose and an end in sight to the extra effort.

Low-Bar Goals

But while the individual stretch goal is an overt cause of disengagement and is quite ineffective in the long run, the *low-bar* (too easy) goal is the most insidious cause of inefficiency. The leaders never find out that the goal is too easy because nobody is willing to tell them. And the fact that the goal is too easy is often not obvious, because due to variation in the work, some people hit the goal on some days and some people don't.

Take, for example, the case of a hotel's housekeeping team. We were once asked to develop a case study for a hotel management team that needed to deliver a training event for its leaders. We decided to use the hotel's housekeeping operation as an example, and so we gathered some real data about the process. When we asked one of the senior leaders how long it took to clean a room, he said "32 minutes"—such an exact number that we thought someone must have recently done a time study. Nope.

When we asked to see the data, we heard something like, "No, silly, the goal is 15 rooms cleaned per attendant per day, so 480 minutes divided by 15 rooms is 32 minutes per room." Sounds like napkin math in reverse, doesn't it?

As consultants, if there's one thing we know anything about, it's staying in hotels. And having experienced at least a few times the need to wait outside while a housekeeper cleaned our rooms, we knew one thing for sure: there's no way that it takes 32 minutes to clean a typical hotel room! The goal of 15 rooms per day had to be too low.

We designed the case study and delivered the training class for the leaders, challenging them to rethink the housekeeping process; and the members of one hotel's team decided to go back and actually do the housekeeping project at their property. They measured the room cleaning process, and sure enough the 15-room goal was too low to motivate anyone. They discovered that housekeepers were even exerting peer pressure on one another to not exceed the goal, since nobody wanted the company to increase it.

After streamlining the process, with solutions including creating different processes for "stay-over" rooms compared with "checkout" cleaning, the team identified new standards for quality of cleaning and the time required to clean each type of room, and it created a new variable incentive plan (still an individual goal, but a better one on a sliding scale). Performance improved dramatically.

Often the individual goal actually becomes a place to *stop*, which brings to mind a great story about a "10-mile" run that we heard from a soldier who attended the U.S. Army's Special Forces Qualification Course in 1992. The Q-course, as it was called back then, may be the toughest training and evaluation experience in the world; and while it's very physical, it's even more mental. The candidates were told that they would have to complete a 10-mile run as a team and that there would be a truck at the finish line for them to get into for the ride home.

The team arrived intact at the finish line, but as the team approached the truck, it began to pull away slowly. It stayed within sight of them, but it kept going... for another 16 miles. A number of candidates quit running that day and were dropped from the course. The funny thing was that all of them were in shape to complete a marathon, if they had only known that the goal was 26 miles instead of 10.

Individual Accountabilities with Team Goals

As we proceed, we'll discuss ways to hold team members individually accountable for their individual performance while driving improved overall results by setting team goals. We'll dedicate a future chapter to measuring individual work standards, which are different from goals because they're based on *actual* current performance capability instead of *desired* performance. Another chapter will discuss the appropriate formation of team goals that are customer oriented, similar to the example in the previous Installation story.

As we've demonstrated with the examples in this chapter, individual goals are often actually counterproductive, either driving the wrong behaviors or failing to drive the right ones. In contrast, Engaged *Team* Performance leverages the power of *team*work to drive *teams* of people to achieving *team* goals, while still holding individuals accountable for meeting appropriate performance standards. And consequentially, ETP gets much better (and much more sustainable!) results than individual goals do. We'll discuss how to do all that in Chapters 8 and 9.

The bottom line is that Engaged Team Performance is all about setting and attaining *team* goals. Otherwise, we'd have called it "Engaged Individual Performance" and marketed it to golfers.

Chapter Summary

+ Individual goals don't always work very well.

+ Sometimes individual goals drive unintended behaviors, like increased activities that don't add value for customers.

+ Individual stretch goals don't motivate people in the long term.

+ The worst kind of individual goals are the ones that are too low.

+ Individual goals sometimes distract organizations from the important realization that customers only feel the team's performance: the individuals may win, but the team may still lose.

5

Is It Process or Performance? Both!

"It's the process, not the people!" Or is it??

W E HAVE ALREADY explained that the power of Engaged
Team Performance comes from combining both process and performance excellence. While this might seem to be a fairly easy-
to-believe concept, many popular improvement methods have
recently focused so much on the process that the performance side
got overlooked. We have actually contributed to that misconcep-
tion as well, through our involvement in writing books like *The
Six Sigma Way* that were successful particularly because *process
improvement alone actually works*. Unfortunately, some very successful process improvement projects have failed to sustain performance over time and have left some possible value unclaimed.
Process improvement and performance improvement together
deliver game-changing results.

In our past roles as process improvement facilitators, we
were often invited to visit a business area, assess the process,
and try to find ways to improve it. In the past, we would always

start by saying, "Now remember, problems are caused by processes, not people." For the most part, this was true.

And when we would first ask why the process is the way it is, we would almost always hear, "It's always been that way." (And a few times, we've heard, "Well, we just implemented this new computer system last year that messed it all up . . .")

Most of the time, the process is just a product of its long history. And often the process was incrementally changed as a response to specific events, rather than strategically implemented for optimum results. So a neutral set of eyes, from either an external consultant or an internal process improvement expert, can often see opportunities and foster changes to drive an improved result. Here's basically how that approach works.

The process grows along with the company, and it changes over time. Often, a new problem or issue creates a rework loop to fix problems or a need for an additional step to check work. People come up with good ideas and implement them. Eventually, the process is disconnected from the customer and is complicated with too many handoffs, checks, and errors. The people who live within the process are comfortable with the incremental decisions that were made over time, and so they're blind to some of the potential opportunities.

Then, someone decides to have lunch with a consultant (internal, external, or both)!

The consultant sells an engagement by comparing the client's performance with some "benchmarks" of other similar organizations. Sometimes the consultant uses a napkin to calculate the team's efficiency using a "magic equation."

The consultant then comes into the company and asks the client's employees, "What is the process, and why is it done that way?" over and over, in different ways and applying new measurements as needed, until they all understand the current state of the process, the customer requirements, and the performance gaps.

The consultant applies some tried-and-true data analysis and workflow streamlining theories in order to isolate root causes and recommend specific solutions, hopefully also engaging client team members to generate some of the ideas too, in order to get their buy-in along the way.

The client leadership team approves and implements some of the consultant's and internal team's recommendations, usually driving at least enough financial impact to pay for the consultant and the work the team invested in the change process.

The client leaders and team members follow through to put documentation, work control measures, and accountabilities in place in order to maintain the gain.

Generally, process improvement works very well, for both the client and the consultant. Of course, as with anything else, there are good, bad, and evil consultants, and some clients have had good experiences with implementing change and some haven't. But nobody can argue with the beneficial impact that process improvement has had upon efficiency and effectiveness in the last few decades.

Higher productivity is probably the only way the world could have so vastly improved our standard of living in the last 25 years without (recently) seeing runaway price inflation. Basically, we get more value for our money than we used to. Anyone who has a couple of laptop computers, an iPod or two, and a large flat-screen TV lying around the house knows what we mean: even 10 years ago that stuff was much more expensive than it is today.

So, what explains the productivity improvement?

✦ *Technology.* Information technology, automation, and controls have improved everything from stoplight waiting time (do you know what those wires under the road at intersections do? They sense whether your car needs the light to change, and they weren't around 25 years ago) to self-service gas pumps, airline ticket booking, etc. Technology is ubiquitous; we often take it for granted, and it really does improve our lives.

◆ *Global competition.* Some would lament the facts that the world economy is moving jobs overseas and that the cost of making those computers, TVs, and MP3 players is just staying under control through labor rate competition. But the cost of almost everything has pretty much stayed under control for a long while, even when the U.S. Federal Reserve and other central banks put loose money out there for most of the last decade. And remember, 70 percent of our economy is service, not manufacturing. Services aren't so easy to provide from afar. So, cheaper global labor rates reduce comparative cost, and global competition forces us to drive more productivity internally in order to compete.

◆ *Lean Six Sigma.* If you hadn't heard of this funny-sounding improvement methodology before picking up this book and reading the previous chapters, you may have been living under a rock. Someone even named a GI Joe action figure set after it a few years ago. Many companies have implemented these methods well, a number have tried and failed, and some are still just getting into all of it, but you'd be hard-pressed to find a company out there that hasn't tried some kind of process improvement. Again, that's a vast change from 25 years ago, and much of the credit can go to this approach and its precursors, Total Quality Management (TQM) and the Toyota Production System (TPS).

As we said in Chapter 1, the main point of this book is that *current productivity gains are only the tip of the iceberg.*

There's a lot more opportunity left out there to harvest. As we've already discussed, we encounter vast productivity potential even in companies that have already studied and improved some processes. And some of the opportunities are still process issues, disconnects between the work and the customer, or simply "the way we've always done it" that hasn't kept up with advances in technology or theory.

But equally as many of the opportunities are in *performance* instead of process, and that's where we'd encourage everyone to do some self-examination. When we study a department at a client company, we often find that people are delivering two to three hours of "productive work" in an eight-hour day, just like the people in the GPS department were doing in the story we told in the Prologue.

If you don't believe that, time *yourself* someday. You'll notice some of the typical process waste in your day—for example, answering phone calls about the status of your work, waiting at the printer, and double-checking your (or others'!) work. And then between chatting, breaks, lunch, and a little surfing of the Internet, you'll find that you can fritter away much of the rest of the day. Ask yourself: "What did I actually produce today, and how much work time did that really consume?"

We're not saying that people should keep their noses to the grindstone for eight full hours every day, but perhaps five would be reasonable? Seriously, we're happy with five.

So, here's an editorial with a challenge for everyone: if you believe in positive change and are willing to answer the call to sacrifice for the common good, let's all start with putting in a full day's work every day. Then use technology and process improvement to work even smarter tomorrow than you did yesterday. And don't put too much of your excess energy into complaining, fighting your employer's priorities, worrying about labor rates paid by foreign competition, or sticking to your "work rules" to protect jobs. Unions everywhere from the airlines to the auto manufacturers have recently learned that protecting some jobs yesterday can sometimes mean losing all the jobs today. So bargain with your employer all you want, but when you're at work, just do your job as well as you can for your customer, your employer, and your own self-respect.

Losing the Six Sigma Way

After just proclaiming the value of Lean Six Sigma and comparable approaches *in general* in driving some past efficiency and effectiveness gains, we now need to qualify that a bit. It hasn't worked out perfectly for everyone.

It starts with the greatest of intentions. An executive, usually one who spent some time at General Electric or another of the early adopters of the improvement methodologies, decides to introduce Six Sigma to his or her new organization. The senior team hears about the potential benefits, and the principles make great sense; who could argue with running the business by focusing on customers, understanding processes, and making data-based decisions? And besides, it has a cool brand name: *Six Sigma*.

But soon, the mom-and-apple-pie optimism meets the cold reality of the corporate bureaucracy needed to launch it quickly. GE took eight years—nobody has time for that.

So first, the company starts its search for a "deployment champion" from outside. Management interviews numerous "master black belts"—many of them seem to have been *trained* as master black belts, but can only produce green belt certifications for some reason. The person selected has good credentials based on having led at least two projects at a previous employer and is eager to lead his or her first Six Sigma deployment.

Management often finds a consulting company to help with the deployment as well. This isn't hard. Those companies are a dime a dozen. It seems that a herd of professional trainers decided in the last decade that the Total Quality Management movement was declining and that Lean Six Sigma was the next wave, so there's lots of supply. The trouble is that it's hard to tell the good ones from the bad. Luckily, a former GE guy in procurement knows something about Six Sigma and has a "friend" in a consulting company, and so somehow the competitive bidding process gets sidetracked so that the deployment can get started quickly.

Of course, the consulting company is really a training company anyway (or even worse, a software company pretending to be a training company), and so the deployment strategy soon becomes a "sheep-dip training" with integrated e-learning for hundreds of project leaders without identifying any really important projects for all of them to lead. Everyone gets certified with projects that have titles like "Should I put my stapler on the right side of the desk or the left?" and then these folks immediately start interviewing for Six Sigma deployment leader roles at other companies. Or they get jobs in procurement.

And after all the education, projects, and infrastructure are in place, someone has the gall to say, "Lean Six Sigma doesn't work," and is quickly proved wrong. For, of course, out of the myriad projects the project leaders started, a few (usually 15 percent or so) get finished and get fantastic results. Just think of the results they'd have had if they'd worked on the right projects, dedicated appropriate resources, and held people accountable!

The really funny thing is that Six Sigma really *does* work, especially when combined with other good tools from Lean enterprise, Reengineering, and organizational design. Oriented to the right opportunities, it gets great results. And perhaps even less shockingly, it works best in the hands of an experienced practitioner rather than a new trainee. The real trouble is that all the experienced practitioners are so busy training trainees that they're hard to find and hard to retain.

So, perhaps a few universal truths about Lean Six Sigma:

+ Something that seems too good to be true probably is. If you're not at GE, simply copying "what GE did" is likely going to be a recipe for frustration.

+ Sheep-dip training doesn't work. People and projects have to be selected very carefully in order to develop effective practitioners of a tool set that includes change management, process analysis, and heavy statistics. It's not for everyone.

+ Lean Six Sigma practitioners are expensive because they deliver great value. If they are good practitioners, the market (perhaps eventually a consulting company) finds them and puts them to work on important project opportunities for someone else, or even has them work on delivering expensive Lean Six Sigma training, supported by cool software.

+ There is still plenty of improvement opportunity available in companies, and Lean Six Sigma tools could contribute substantially if deployed appropriately.

We hope that's not all bad news. And we hope that all the companies that are trying to follow the *Six Sigma Way* find their way back onto the path!

$R = Q \times A$

A key point, though, is that Lean Six Sigma usually works pretty well for managing processes and not so well for managing people. Dyed-in-the-wool believers will tell you that's not true: they'll swear that if it's "done right," the data will manage the people. But taking some liberties with the anti-gun-control slogan, "Data doesn't manage people. People manage people." And it's even better when they manage themselves.

Improving the process will only get you so far. At some point, you also have to drive the right performance within the process. In order to do that, the people have to use the data and the process to *manage their own performance*! Taking that concept to the next level is what Engaged Team Performance is all about.

In the hypothetical equation $R = Q \times A$, *results* (*R*) are equal to the product of the *technical quality* (*Q*) of the process or solution times the *acceptance* (*A*) generated within the people who do the work. It's not a real equation, of course, but the concept is quite powerful. And it underscores the idea that employee buy-in can't be generated by a bunch of statistics or even by a strong project manager . . . it takes a *leader*, along with the right tools and approach.

Process and Performance Improvement at GPS

The Group Proposal Services (GPS) story introduced in the Prologue provides a perfect case in point for seeing the power of combining a good process solution with employee buy-in. As we proceed in this book, we'll refer to GPS routinely as a case study for the concepts that we're illustrating.

As the GPS process improvement project started in 2006, the initial process and data analysis yielded a number of process opportunities, mostly related to handoffs that were later consolidated so that one person could do the whole job. This change reduced some redundant work, and after a short period of cross-training and piloting, the department was able to implement the new process across all its quoting teams. At the point the process changes were fully implemented, the department redeployed 11 temporary employees from the process to other work outside the department (a 17.5 percent reduction in labor). The remaining 54 people, including 4 leaders, were then reorganized into 6 teams.

We'll discuss the process improvement project, which is really only the first half of the GPS story, in Chapter 6, but first, we'll address the performance improvements.

As we have said, strong technical analysis is critical for deciding how to optimally change processes, but acceptance of that change effort is even more important for improving and sustaining performance over time.

Most important for GPS, leaders in the department engaged the team members in designing the changes and then followed through after their process improvements by emplacing work controls, daily data displays, and new team norms regarding collaboration. Leaders updated the charts every day with work volumes, productivity, and customer measures (turnaround time, etc.). The data charts were essential tools to drive performance, as any Lean Six Sigma believer would correctly argue, but the charts alone did not deliver the performance improvement. The charts were critical in allowing the team and the leaders to compare their performance with what the performance *should be* so that the people could *manage their own performance.* Leaders then had to foster that self-management environment and attitude. As we proceed, we'll tell that story in detail and clearly show the difference.

As we'll see in Chapter 8, the definition of the "should-be" performance efficiency standard is not the same thing as a goal. Instead, we call it "standard work time." It's the measured work time that it takes a fully qualified associate to accomplish the task, under regular work conditions. It's not a goal; it's an expectation. The theories involving goals are quite old, yet still true. W. Edwards Deming shared much of those thoughts with the world a long time ago. That hasn't stopped many organizations from implementing harmful individual stretch goals, though, as we discussed in the last chapter.

The basic ETP principle is simple: *if you use data to right-size the team for its work volume and then ask the team to pull together to get all the work done right and on time for the customer, the team will become efficient.* Give credit only for completed "things" that the customer wants and are done right. Rather than creating stretch goals that are by definition just out of reach, the Engaged Team Performance method sets standards that are *just within reach* and then expects teams to figure out how to work together to deliver them consistently.

So we'll be the first to admit that many of the GPS leaders' follow-through actions were just examples of good implementation of a "process control" plan, which we'll discuss in more detail later.

But the real driver of the difference in performance in GPS was the collaboration that the leadership team purposefully drove. Rather than setting only individual metrics, the team leaders focused first on setting and driving *team* metrics. To start that mindset change, the leaders had to change both the work processes and the teams' perceptions about "my work and your work"—eventually everyone had to realize that it was all "our" work.

Some simple yet specific collaborative work practices (norms) needed to be changed: initially, each team member was aligned with a single field office, usually doing only that office's quotes and rarely helping anyone else. The team members initially believed that it was too hard to learn another field office's preferences, so there was an artificial barrier to collaboration. Unfortunately, the inherent daily variation in incoming work would guarantee that a person would be too busy one day and not busy enough the next. Once they established the importance of sharing work, the team members cross-trained to allow multiple people within a team to support each office. Each team made a matrix to track its training status. We'll discuss this integration of collaborative processes and team goals in much more detail in a later chapter.

More Key Mindset Changes

Many leaders are forced to consider opportunities to cut costs by decreasing their departments' service levels. For example, they may try to save money by promising a 10-day turnaround time instead of a 5-day commitment to customers. When we're asked to help with that kind of thing, it can be a tough conversation for us.

The point seems intuitive, but it's dead wrong. *Faster is cheaper*, and slower is more expensive.

Think of it this way: if you extend the deadline from 5 to 10 days to do a 30-minute task, people will just wait 9 days instead of 4 to start doing the work! The task still takes just as much work time if you do it on day 9 as it did on day 4. It's like gravity—what goes up must come down. Work that comes in must go out. Waiting longer to do a task won't make it easier to do when it actually comes time to do it.

Indeed, leaving a customer request sitting for an extra five days just allows people to sort the work a few more times, can let facts and information change, and generates a few "Where's my _____?" phone calls from the customer that have to be answered. All of that actually takes *extra* time. In fact, it's *less* efficient to increase the service time!

While leading a technical support team at SAP, Eric Wansong described this same concept quite aptly for his customer support technicians: "We're not making wine here. Support cases do not get better with age; they tend to turn to vinegar."

The best time to do a 30-minute task is in the 30 minutes immediately after it arrives. The best time to work on a quote that arrives today is . . . today! Lean theorists call this concept "just in time" (JIT). Waiting time is always bad.

The members of the GPS team had an opportunity to apply that key concept when their project first started. Since they were supposed to get quotes turned around within two days from arrival, they had a name for anything that arrived today: *tomorrow's work*! This came from their experiences with individual goals, and the logic was probably something like:

+ Something that arrives today is "due" two days from now.

+ As a Sales Support Specialist, I have to do 15 quotes per day (my "goal").

+ Due to the inherent variation in incoming volume, I'm not sure how many quotes will come in tomorrow from my field office (sometimes it's even zero!).

+ Since I only usually do work for this one field office, I have to save 15 of its quotes to do tomorrow, or I won't make my goal tomorrow.

◆ Therefore, anything that comes in today is tomorrow's work, and I'm probably going to slow down or stop today after I finish 15 quotes.

The individual measurement and goals had actually created work habits that were getting in the way of productivity! Changing to a customer-focused team goal (24-hour turnaround time) eventually allowed the leadership to shift that mindset.

One of the things that the leaders had to do was to correct that terminology every time they heard it, saying something like: "If it arrived today, why isn't it *today's work*?!" Over the few months that the changes were put in place, some of the best peer leaders and role models turned out to be the Sales Support Specialists who had helped to do the process analysis with the project team. These team members were the ambassadors of change to their teammates, and their buy-in stemmed from being involved from the beginning in planning the transformation.

After the changes, the team was measured on how many quotes were *left* at the end of the day, with the intention to sustain a number less than the team's daily production volume (i.e., get the process cycle time under 24 hours so that something that arrives today gets done by tomorrow). Creating intolerance for backlog was the hardest part of the mindset to change, but once people understood the greater value of getting things done sooner, for both the customer and themselves, the team members came together behind their new goal.

The GPS Results

The combination of process changes and Engaged Team Performance techniques quickly got the teams to reliably deliver 24-hour turnaround times, and eventually they even started measuring those times in hours instead of days. Customer satisfaction, which had sometimes been a sore spot for the teams in the past, dramatically increased.

As time went by, the teams' performance and efficiency kept slowly improving, and as the regular attrition of people moving out of the department for various reasons occurred, those people didn't need to be replaced. A few years later, the process was operating at the same original volume of work, but with 38 people instead of 65, which was a 41 percent reduction in total labor! And that number was eerily similar to the number we had written on the napkin in the restaurant back in 2006 before the project started.

Process changes alone had driven 17 percent improvement in efficiency, but Engaged Team Performance was the key to the other 24 percent gained. Lean Six Sigma tools were essential to getting almost halfway there, but ETP took the process to the next level. The teams eventually reduced overhead (leadership and support infrastructure) in addition to variable labor costs as they made the transition to a more streamlined organization. We'll illustrate all those impacts as we move forward . . .

Chapter Summary

+ Process and performance are equally important.

+ Performance improvement trends have not kept up with the great strides seen in process improvement in the last decade.

+ But also in the last decade, some organizations have had frustrating experiences with process improvement methods that have left some promises unfulfilled.

In the Group Proposal Services improvement journey, the score was:

+ Total efficiency improvement: 41 percent
+ Process efficiency improvement: 17 percent
+ Performance efficiency improvement: 24 percent

We will tell the story from both perspectives as we proceed.

Changing Process: The GPS Story and the Power of Lean Six Sigma

Aᴛᴛᴇʀ ɢɪᴠɪɴɢ ʙᴏᴛʜ credit and criticism to the Lean Six Sigma process improvement approach, we thought we should dedicate a short discussion to what it is, how to do it, and why it works. We'll keep it fairly concise, and we've focused the discussion on details about the GPS case that reinforce the power of the methodology. We beg the indulgence of those of you who are already familiar with the methods to resist the urge to skip on to the next chapter. Lean Six Sigma is an important part of the ETP approach!

For those of you who want the full how-to version, however, we'd recommend you pick up one of our previous books, *The Six Sigma Way* by Peter Pande, Robert Neuman, and Roland Cavanagh or the practitioner's handbook, the *Six Sigma Way Team Fieldbook* (the same authors in the same name order). In this chapter, we'll simply tell the story of the Group Proposal Services (GPS) project within the typical approach framework, known by the acronym DMAIC, which stands for Define, Measure, Analyze, Improve, and Control. Without further ado . . .

Define

The GPS department creates quotes for group health, dental, life, and disability products. The department receives approximately 300 requests for quotes daily from its partners in the field sales force. In 2006, the expected turnaround time (TAT) for producing a quote was 48 hours, and in normal situations the team was able to meet that goal 80 to 95 percent of the time, depending on volumes.

In the prior year's "busy season" of 2005 (September–November), however, the team had experienced a drop in its service levels, missing the TAT goal consistently, which was attributed by leaders at the time to the fact that volumes had exceeded the team's capacity. The leaders wanted to ensure that 2006 turned out better.

To kick off the engagement, the department leader wrote an e-mail to her leadership team, and yes, this is the real e-mail text:

Hey, gang! I wanted to provide an email introduction to each other and high-level expectations around your time availability for the next couple weeks.

Dept leaders—First you are an awesome group! Thanks, once again, for being open to examination. I know your passion in wanting to have a slick process where all of your employees have an opportunity to succeed. It's nice to be able to do this review at a time when your inventory is not out-of-control. But you know it is coming again in the fall so this is the time to figure out the next level of improvements. Your participation is an important element of success in this review so have a calendar that is adjustable over the next couple weeks and also start planning having some of your employees available also. Please make a commitment to availability at any time the consulting team is on-site with 24 hours notice in advance.

The department leadership identified an internal project leader, three assistant managers, and a number of Sales Support Specialists (SSSs) to form a team. In the initial team meeting, we facilitated a visioning exercise that invoked the principles of Lean flow. Some of the thoughts on the flip chart were:

+ "Once & Done" processing (no repeat touch)
+ No redundant work; minimum touch
+ "Do It Right the First Time"
+ Capacity matched to demand
+ Rational handoffs versus specialization (hand off only when we have to)
+ Workforce engagement
+ Scalable to demand and variation
+ Team measures, goals, and accountabilities

All those things seemed reasonable, but nobody was sure how *possible* they were. So even though many of the team members knew the process by heart, they agreed to make a high-level process map called a SIPOC (an acronym that stands for suppliers-inputs-process-outputs-customers) and then job-shadow real SSSs to watch the process in action.

At a high level, the process was:

+ The GPS department created quotes for group health, dental, life, and disability products.

+ GPS received approximately 300 requests for quotes daily from its partners in the field sales force, and it returned the quotes to those partners within 48 hours (a key customer requirement).

+ When the requests for quote (RFQs) were received, they were printed and inspected to decide if they were "rush" or "standard" requests. Standard requests went to a queue for processing the next day ("tomorrow's work"), and rush requests were sent for immediate processing.

+ A specialist (SSS) then "prepped" a batch of quotes, by looking up key information (e.g., demographics of the new prospective customer).

+ Next, another specialist reviewed the RFQ and created a "prep sheet" for data entry, using a word processor template that was designed to capture the appropriate information that would need to be entered into the system.

+ The prep sheets went into a queue for Consolidated Data Entry team members (CDEs—usually temporary employees) to enter into the company's computer-generated proposal system.

+ The CDE then placed the completed quote in an electronic folder for the field office to retrieve, and sent an e-mail to tell the office that the entry had been completed, attaching any important notes that the sales team needed to know.

+ After the quote was entered into the system, the paperwork was sent to Post Tracking (another group of temporary employees), who tracked the quote and some pertinent performance information that the department needed (turnaround time, etc.) in another database called Full Service Log.

Like many processes, there were a number of steps with hand-offs to different people, and there were quite a few acronyms, tools, and systems in use in the department! As you probably know from your own company, that's typical too.

The next step was to look at the customer requirements to make sure the process was designed for success. Obviously, the customers wanted their quotes to be timely, accurate, and complete. They seemed happy with the 48-hour turnaround standard, though there were some anecdotal issues about "quality" that were somewhat disputed.

Like most good departments, GPS regularly solicited feedback from customers in the field, and it kept track of complaints and issues as it resolved them. The Pareto chart in Figure 6-1 shows some of the complaints that GPS had received lately and had internally categorized. The department was not sure that every issue was being reported, but 160 complaints out of thousands of quotes wasn't too bad. The team had a passionate discussion of the "read your mind" error, which seemed to mean that the field offices believed that GPS should know certain preferences without being told, and one person complained that every field office wanted it to be Burger King (from the old commercial, "Have it your way...").

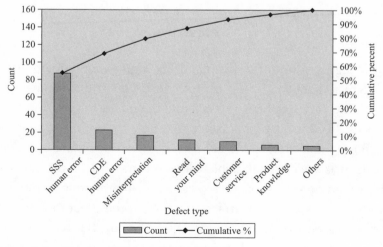

Figure 6-1   Pareto Chart of Feedback

GPS had previously created a "benefit map" to capture the different preferences for each sales rep and field office, and the expectation was that the SSS would know the office's preferences and apply them appropriately—for example, even if a broker (the field office's customer) had specified only certain provisions in the request for quote, the SSS was expected to know if, when, and how to apply the field office's preferences to provide additional information that the broker hadn't specified. It seemed quite complicated! Hence, the SSS team members were convinced that only one person could service each field office effectively.

There was also a general opinion that "reducing and standardizing the options offered" to the customer would allow better sharing of work. When someone referred to this idea as making "vanilla quotes," the department leader seemed very displeased. But the Lean Six Sigma approach very clearly encourages people to understand and try to *meet* customers' needs, not start by trying to negotiate them down; and so after some offline recalibration within the leadership team, the project team continued along with the general agreement that the team would need to try to maintain the policy of meeting the individual preferences of each field office. The project team also decided to measure the impact of those preferences before trying to make a decision.

Measure

Drawing from both the Lean and Six Sigma methodologies, the GPS team needed to measure both the process flow (using a Lean tool called a Value Stream Map) and the inherent variation in the process (a core Six Sigma concept).

The Value Stream Map (VSM) is shown in Figure 6-2. Some Lean purists reading this book will most certainly note that the team missed putting some of the typical VSM information on the map. If you're interested in learning more about this great tool, pick up *Learning to See* by Mike Rother and John Shook. But we can assure you that the project still saved the company over $1 million even

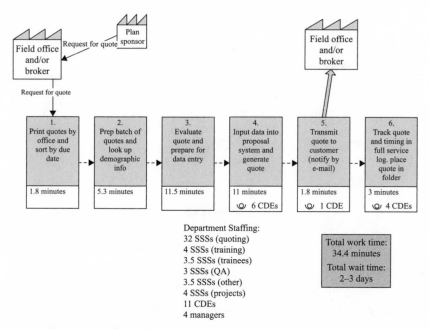

Figure 6-2   Produce Quotes

without all the proper symbols and data. Actually, the person who captured the map started by trying to make it look like the original, which was made of Post-it notes across a conference room wall. Post-it notes are the best "software" we've ever used!

The Value Stream Map takes a traditional process map and adds critical information about the process directly to it, creating a single visual picture of the process that can be quite useful for analysis. Some of the typical information types are:

+ Value of each process step
+ Staffing for each process step (in FTE*)

*FTE is an acronym for *full-time equivalent*. It's calculated by adding up the amount of time each person works in a year, then dividing by the number of work hours in a standard year (2,080). This allows comparison of staffing levels when some full-time and some part-time employee schedules are mixed together. For example, two 20-hour-per-week part-time employees together make one FTE.

+ Volume flow rate of customer demand for products or services
+ Work time to do each step
+ Work in process (inventory) waiting before each step
+ Wait time in each inventory queue
+ Information flow to control work

Analyze

After gathering a plethora of data, the team needed to apply both process and data analysis techniques to understand the reasons for the current state of the process.

A quick study of the previous month's quote volume showed some interesting daily variation. Obviously, with a required two-day turnaround time, the team couldn't be sized for the average volume, since some days were much heavier than others. The daily variation looked as it does in Figure 6-3. The volume charts show that the average daily volume was 311, but the typical expected range of potential daily volumes (about 3 standard deviations) was +/−100!

A box plot analysis, shown in Figure 6-4, by day of the week helped to illuminate one key cause, light Fridays.

While we won't discuss every data chart that the GPS team produced and analyzed, we will highlight one more critical piece

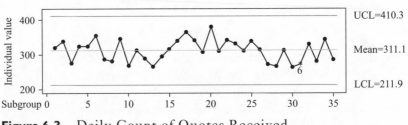

Figure 6-3   Daily Count of Quotes Received

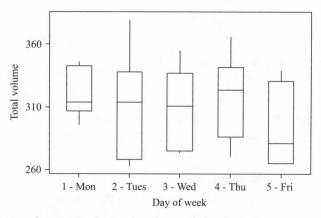

Figure 6-4   Quote Volume by Day of the Week

of information: work time. The GPS team had actually already done a time study before the project started. The team had gathered both the work time and the attributes of individual quotes, which allowed the project team to calculate the average time for the SSSs and data entry CDEs to do the main work in processing a quote: 29.6 minutes, just as the department leader had said from the beginning.

The team quickly collected data from the other players in the process—for example, the CDEs doing printing and tracking tasks. All of it made it onto the Value Stream Map. The team members had some great conversations along the way as they created the VSM. To paraphrase some highlights:

"Prepping is helping without really helping," one of the Specialists said. She was referring to Step 2, the way that some SSSs would try to help another team member who was swamped. Because they didn't know the other person's office preferences, they couldn't help by doing a whole quote. But they could do some of the menial demographic data lookup work at the beginning of the quoting task.

It turned out that the help didn't really help, due to a behavioral and accountability issue. "Yeah, I have to admit that I check the information anyway, after someone preps for me," another SSS replied. "After all, the quote has my name on it, so it's me who would get in trouble if it's wrong." It sounded like the prepping step was redundant.

"But what else could we help with? It's all because of the differences in the office preferences and benefit maps. If the offices would just standardize what they want, we'd be able to help each other with complete quotes, but it's so hard to learn each office's preferences that prepping is the only way we can help each other." Back to vanilla quotes again . . .

This conversation revealed that the preferences were actually *all already written down*. Each office had submitted a preference template with all of its preferences listed. So the project team decided to just measure the feared effect of having to learn a new office's preferences. The team gave a "benefit map" from a specific field office to an SSS who didn't support that office, and the team timed her while she did some quotes. The first few took 5 to 10 minutes longer than normal. After that, she did them almost as fast as that office's regular SSS. The team realized that it was potentially painful and stressful to cross-train, perhaps, but certainly not impossible.

Another fairly obvious handoff problem had a more insidious cause. "What about the CDEs and the data entry?" another person asked. "That template that the SSS fills out has exactly the same information as the proposal system that the CDEs use; why didn't we just have the SSS enter it into the system directly and skip the CDE altogether?"

"Oh, there was a good reason for that . . . [There always is!] Originally, the computer proposal system was underpowered and very slow. It didn't make sense for an expensive resource like the SSS to be tied up waiting for screens to update during data entry. And when we ran into capacity issues last fall, we found that we could hire temps and teach them the proposal system pretty quickly, whereas it's hard to teach SSSs their whole job—they really have to know a lot about products. So with the CDEs we could more quickly react to volume changes." They had missed the obvious point that the CDE was doing a completely redundant role, now that the system speed issue had been fixed.

But that brought up another question: "What happened last fall anyway?"

"Well, our volumes increased dramatically, and we got behind. Like all organizations, we occasionally have some attrition, and we were in the midst of training some new people we had hired to replace some experienced people who had moved on to other roles in the company. Our people get promotions into other departments partly because the SSS role is such a great place to learn the company's product line. Then when new folks are in training, we have to check 100 percent of their work, which takes extra time."

A measurement of the actual volumes quickly verified that the dramatic "50 percent volume spike" was a bit of an urban legend. The volume increase during the last busy season had been about 10 percent, the same as that of the two previous years. It was true that they'd gotten behind, but it had been caused by the capacity constraints due to the normal attrition and training issues that had just happened at the wrong time, right before the busy season. When capacity doesn't meet demand, a team can get behind fast. And then it takes even more work to keep up once the "Where's my quote?" phone call questions start coming in.

The members of the team felt bad about their past issues, and they were truly dedicated to having a better busy season in the coming fall. They finished the Analyze phase with some good ideas.

Improve

The process changes that the team implemented were fairly obvious and straightforward. Basically, the team cut out all the handoffs and had the SSSs do the entire quote from start to finish and then track their own data in the tracking database.

This meant that the SSS team would have to be trained on using the proposal-generating system for data entry and also the tracking system (Full Service Log). A few team members reluctantly volunteered to try it, and by the following week they decided that they never wanted to go back to the old process. The new way was much faster.

To continue to prove the concept, the project team enlisted the support of the existing Midwest team to pilot the changes. Six team members, many who had participated in the project team's analysis meetings as well, were trained on the systems and began to process quotes the new way. The new process had fewer steps, as shown in Figure 6-5.

We shouldn't minimize the effort that it took to pilot the process with the Midwest team, make small changes to the plan, and then cross-train and reorganize an entire department over a whole summer. It was a Herculean task, and the GPS team had its ups and downs but stayed focused on being ready for the busy season in the fall.

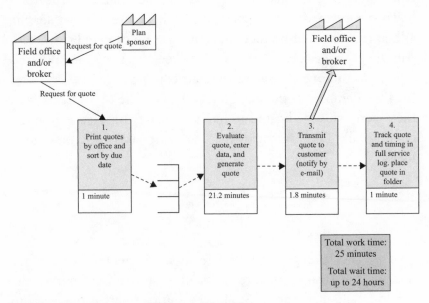

Figure 6-5   Produce Quotes (New Process)

The team hit that busy season with 11 fewer people (after the temporary employees in CDE roles were redeployed elsewhere) and had no service or backlog issues. The project was a smashing success. The field offices noticed that their quotes were being returned much faster, and they also saw fewer errors, which was another consequence of the reduction of handoffs. The people had worked very hard to change, and many of them later said that the summer was a very difficult time, but they'd do it again in a heartbeat.

Control

As we discussed in the previous chapter, one of the key differences in delivering upon the promise of Engaged Team Performance lies in the approach and vigor dedicated to implementing the Control phase.

Like too many teams do, the GPS team almost lost its way on the path to the Control phase. It started out with the best of intentions. The department leader, from the very beginning of the project, wanted to drive data-based decision making into the team's culture. So even as the project team was in the middle of implementing the process changes during the summer, it scheduled a planning session to discuss Control measures.

Here is an excerpt of the department leader's message to the team at the time:

> . . . *I do have an expectation that certain topics will be addressed during the day and that one or more of you will be on-point for specific topics . . .*

> ✦ *Be prepared with the straw-man control charts or at least the current state. When Dodd Starbird visited with us briefly about control mechanisms, he had provided a template regarding components of control charts (source, reason for control, etc.). In addition, I would like to see some preliminary results.*

+ *Please be prepared regarding any current or planned changes and your expectation around the quality/training component of the GPS process.*

+ *Be prepared with an updated understanding of any project milestones or challenges.*

You've all done a super job in executing some big changes; let's get this last piece of Control nailed. This, to me, is the most exciting part of all (and not because it's the numbers stuff). This is what makes the process sustainable and what makes the improvements a way of life.

She was dead-on right, and her vision for sustainable performance measurement was critical to the team's later success. But for all the great intentions, the team almost didn't get there.

After a great planning session in the summer, the team was asked to create a package of data charts and begin to post them in the team areas. The department leader scheduled one more follow-up meeting on September 26 to showcase the measures and the new process. She invited a number of her peers—other department leaders in the company who were interested in engaging in similar process improvement efforts and emplacing similar controls. It was intended as a victory tour.

As they started to walk through the facility, the group came around the corner into a team area and found the team's data board. There were no data charts, and there was a single message on it, "Team 3 Rocks!"

The department leader was quite unhappy and a bit embarrassed by the missing charts and the slogan scrawled on the data board that day, but she realized that it would just take a bit more work to get it done. Yet the "Team 3 Rocks!" slogan actually became a rallying cry to finish the Control phase work.

The team had plenty of good reasons for the initial failure: the process changes, a facility move, and the preparations for the September-to-November busy season had all seemed more important. The team had already gotten the gains from the process changes when it redeployed the 11 temporary CDE employees earlier in the summer. And so setting up the performance data charts had seemed to be a longer-term priority.

The department leader stuck to her vision, however, and she made a very clear statement by immediately reassigning one of the three supervisors to be a full-time data analyst to support the Control phase effort. Finally realizing that she was serious about the importance of the data charts, the department teams put the charts up and started using them.

And we found an easy way to remind the leaders about the importance of the performance controls and check on their progress. "How's Team 3 doing?" I would ask. "Team 3 Rocks!" was always the reply, with a wry grin. And Julie Stanley and I still use that greeting four years later.

Without Deb Blackman's persistence and Julie's team's hard work to finish the performance management package, this book probably would never have been written.

It sounds so simple, but it really took weeks of work to identify the right ways to measure the team's process, inputs, and outputs and then set up the system linkages, reports, and analytical tools so that the numbers could be updated and reprinted for display every morning.

Ultimately, the access to the data allowed the team to establish the right team performance measures and goals, which we'll discuss in a later chapter. For now, we'll suffice it to say that Engaged Team Performance can't work without data, and no team we've ever met has had the right data when it started its ETP journey. There is *always* work to be done to establish solid control measures.

Chapter Summary

✦ The Lean Six Sigma process improvement approach typically follows a five-step method: Define, Measure, Analyze, Improve, Control.

✦ In the Group Proposal Services team's Lean Six Sigma project, the project team followed those steps to substantially improve the process.

Power to the People: Facilitation and the Cycle of Change

Before we continue the GPS story to see the team's great results from *performance* improvement, we thought we'd highlight the benefits that strong teamwork can deliver during the initial *process* improvement phase that GPS had just completed. Collaboration, teamwork, and good facilitation will prove to be the keys to Engaged Team Performance, and so starting early during the transformation process is essential. In this chapter, we'll outline key team-building, meeting facilitation, and change adoption principles that will have a critical impact on the success of your ETP undertaking.

Inclusion

Anyone who has participated in a large-scale "business transformation" effort can probably tell you how painful it was. Often those efforts start with a known solution, which could sound like a good thing unless you're one of the people who are being "transformed" by it! Whether designed by a consulting company with past experience doing the same kind of project for other companies (which is often led by a newly minted MBA with a fancy PowerPoint deck from the consulting archives!), or perhaps tailored to the deployment of a new enterprisewide computer system, the solution-first approach can often turn into a poorly executed implementation of a good idea, which then fails when managers try to jam it down the employees' throats. We've seen a few of those failures, and sometimes we've even taken the opportunity to help pick up the pieces in the "business transformation aftermarket" for consulting. It's not pretty.

You see, it's not enough to come up with the right solution. Remember the hypothetical equation that we introduced earlier, $R = Q \times A$? Acceptance (A) is just as important as the technical quality (Q) of the solution. You can probably even think back to a personal situation at work where you were completely right and still lost. That happens all the time to people at home too, so we hear.

The much bigger picture of inclusion is provided by Jean-Marc Gottero, European head of strategy, planning, and development, World Wide Channels of Cisco, who believes that customer value creation calls for a collaborative model. The more that employees feel involved in business projects and decision making, the more value that they will create for their company and thus for the firm's customers. Cisco has been applying this principle since 2003, when it shifted from a command and control model to a participative model for management. The results have been astounding: company revenue has increased 64 percent since 2001.

In order to gain acceptance from the team members who have to live with the final solution, we find that it's best to include them appropriately in the design process. While employees understand that business decisions are not a democracy and they don't always get to vote on the question of "*if* we're going to change," those employees often have valuable perspectives on "*how* best to change" the work processes that they use every day. And even if the employees aren't given free rein to decide everything, they will accept and embrace the new solution if they had an opportunity to be heard. Inclusion in good faith leads to acceptance.

So when we launch an ETP effort within an organization, we choose a team from the department to participate in leading the effort. Keys to assembling a successful team from among a department's workforce are representation, skills, personalities, and size.

For a group of people to meet regularly and effectively for some candid "cuss'n and discuss'n" (as our friend and colleague Carolyn Talasek would say), team size is very important. Too large, and time defeats communication—not everyone can get an opportunity to have his or her perspective heard, and some members shut down or quit coming. Research and personal experience show that a team larger than a "dirty dozen" requires members to have exceptional interpersonal skills and a desire to participate or the group will fail to come together as a unit. "Large numbers of people—by virtue of their size—have trouble interacting constructively as a group, much less agreeing on actionable specifics," say Jon Katzenbach and Douglas Smith in their classic book *The Wisdom of Teams*. Richard Hackman, in his book *Leading Teams*, relates a story of a man who ran a nonprofit whose board of directors numbered 40. When asked what he thought such a large board could accomplish, he replied, "Nothing," in a way that implied he liked it that way.

Logistics can often get in the way too; for example, gaining agreement on a common meeting time and finding a place large enough to contain the group can become problematic. Statements of purpose, recommendations, and action plans become mushy—"designed by committee" becomes an unfortunate reality.

When circumstances warrant a larger team, strong facilitation by a neutral facilitator and a solid agenda become paramount. Such larger teams work best when they are brought together for a single purpose during a very focused time period, for example, a two-day WorkOut meeting. Solid planning can prevent the aforementioned logistical challenges, and the facilitator has to be an expert in "herding cats"; that reminds us of a project we led with seven WorkOut teams looking for cost reductions in a division. We called them "Cost Action Teams," or CATS, for short. That time, we really *were* herding cats . . .

On the other hand (or paw), groups of four or less aren't usually representative of the affected stakeholders, and smaller teams don't seem to be able to build the momentum to deliver lasting results. Small teams lack the capacity both to coalesce interpersonally and to study the topic in enough technical detail. Typically, consensus is easily gained in the room, but is not translatable to the rest of the constituents outside.

The sweet spot seems to be seven or eight members with the right technical and social skills, people who are connected to the work being studied and capable of representing the rest of the producing workers, support teams (for example, the IT, training, and quality assurance departments), and leaders. Along with people who know the work, it is important to include people who have access to the data within the team's systems; sometimes that's a supervisor, and sometimes we need to find a systems analyst or business intelligence expert who can query appropriate information from databases.

Key Team Parameter: Size 5–12 people, with 7–8 optimum

Constructing a team that can speak for all the members' peers can be challenging. Often, everyone wants to participate—no one wants to be left out—but who is going to mind the store? How do we fit everyone in a room?

To address this problem, we try to find a "diagonal slice" through the constituents and stakeholders, gaining both a diversity of expertise in the technical knowledge of the process and a representative selection of the levels of leadership. This means finding people who can represent their peers at their level in the hierarchy while they represent their functional group as well. This kills two birds with one stone. Think about it—six people could theoretically represent six levels and six functional groups at once. That may not always be completely practical, but it's a great vision to start with.

In our example, the GPS project team turned out to be the perfect size, with a couple of leaders, an internal project manager, a trainer, and a few Sales Support Specialists who did both production and quality control work. We brought in other experts when necessary, but the core team was capable of representing the entire department both technically and emotionally.

The War Room

Speaking of fitting the team in a room, we always need a room! It sounds almost amusing, but our consulting team usually makes one seemingly unreasonable demand when we start a project: we want a *dedicated* room. At the outset, the concept seems simple; since we work visually on the walls of the room, creating process maps and other documents on the walls, we want to be able to keep the team's documentation up for a month or two while the team is working.

The team doesn't meet nonstop in the room, of course, and the team's focused activities are probably only happening on two or three days of every week. So, with conference room space in short supply in every company on the planet, we often hear that it's impossibly wasteful to protect a single conference room for a couple of months. But after intense negotiations, we often get a spare conference room, office, utility room, or even (once) a large walk-in coat closet, complete with coat racks!

Once we find and set up a team war room, however, it delivers an added benefit. People in the department realize that our project effort must be *really* important since it got its own room! Believe it or not, that simple fact sends a message to the organization.

The GPS team found a quite unique conference room in its work area: a triangular-shaped room hardly bigger than a closet, with no windows. It was perfect.

The GPS team also benefited from an experiment that the company was running—trying out some new workstation configurations. The new layout included shorter cubicle walls and center-facing "pods" of desks, so that the colocated team members could communicate and collaborate more effectively. We'll discuss that colocation in further detail later, but for now we'll just emphasize that effective design of the work area is a critical enabler of production team collaboration, just as a war room enables a project team to focus on its initiative.

Curmudgeons

As any team comes together, the people within it jockey for position to fill roles. There are always yea-sayers and nay-sayers, comedians and serious people. Though we couldn't find one to add to our team for the GPS effort, one of our favorite personalities for staffing teams is the *curmudgeon*. What's that, you ask? Think of the person that always responds to a new idea with "That'll never work," or, courtesy of an ironworker early in Roland's career, "Screwed again!" An iconic curmudgeon of the last three decades is Andy Rooney of the television news magazine *60 Minutes*. Bushy eyebrows and a contrarian outlook, Andy always has the closing word.

Curmudgeons are a favorite because, although they may not always be well respected by their peers, they are vocal. They have an opinion on everything, almost always intentionally contrary to what they perceive that the management team wants to hear. We often follow the ancient adage "Keep your friends close and your enemies closer," knowing that they will have an opinion about the proceedings and that it is better for them to have heard it firsthand than be repeating hearsay later. We also have found that they tend to be quite polar; once they become a real participant (which usually happens as solutions are being developed), they can become the most outspoken evangelists of the change. How cool is that? Start with vocal resistance and conclude with a strong supporter.

While starting up a process improvement engagement at a refinery in the Northwest, Roland identified a classic curmudgeon in the ranks and invited him to join the project team. He declined. We met with him and pressed. He refused. To our consternation we continued to hear scuttlebutt attributed to him about what a waste of time this effort was going to be and how these consultants were just going to collect a bunch of cash and leave things worse than before. It was strong stuff, and in our experience, likely to get worse as the project progressed.

"Well, if we can't get him on board, we will have to neutralize him," we said to ourselves. We gathered together a coalition of his peers and explained how valuable his input and extensive experience would be to the team's work, and we sent them off to visit with him to ask him to come along. We had given ourselves a win-win situation: if he joined the team, we felt confident we could turn him around; and if he declined again, he'd be less able to complain about the outcome.

"Nope" was still the reply, but now the members of the peer group started feeling that he was letting them down by not joining them, and word got around. His bark was now little more than a yip—an annoyance, but without credibility to the team and the plant. The project succeeded even without the curmudgeon on board.

If you can't get the curmudgeon to join you, make sure the team knows that you really did try. Be conservative though; only one curmudgeon per team.

Finally, be wary of any attempts to stack the deck—when one stakeholder group announces that it needs to have a bunch of people on the team, making the composition lopsided in its favor. Encourage the group members to find key individuals who will bring forth that stakeholder group's issues and keep the rest of their group informed outside of the project meetings.

Key Team Parameter: Select a "diagonal slice" of team members through the hierarchy and functions, even including a curmudgeon.

Meeting Facilitation

How many meetings have you attended where the outcome appeared predetermined, with the meeting leader leading and guiding the discussion with a thinly veiled intent to gain "consensus" or "buy-in" to his or her pet solution? We've been the victim of a few and have come away feeling tricked or sullied as a result. Although the leader may walk away thinking he or she has garnered the support of the attendees, the outcome is usually quite the opposite. "What a sham!" "Watch what happens when I tell the others how that went!" "Who are they trying to fool?" are typical postmeeting hallway and restroom remarks.

As we mentioned in Chapter 2, to improve the effectiveness of collaborative meeting opportunities, General Electric (GE) developed WorkOut through trial and error in the early 1990s and used it very successfully to transform its businesses. As it became more ingrained in GE's culture, the company relaxed the internal controls on the process, and in the late 1990s we witnessed WorkOuts that were just "do it my way" meetings. To GE's credit, this trend has recently been reversed as the company reestablished the important fundamentals. In your organization, you must stay true to the ETP mission in order to avoid similar outcomes. One method of doing so is through neutral facilitation.

Neutral facilitation implies just that: unbiased, evenhanded management of the interaction and discussion, encouraging everyone to speak, even drawing out the silent ones, and frequently politely shutting down the verbose. There are many well-founded techniques and tools available to enable good facilitation, too many for us to delve into here—just do a quick Google search or look at the numerous books on Amazon.

But we do want to say a few words about the neutral facilitator. Team or project leaders often find it difficult to maintain neutrality. They simply have too much suspended on the outcome, and they frequently have mulled the problem over enough so that they have arrived at their own conclusions. Teams instantly detect the leader's bias, even when it's unintentional, and they begin to feel manipulated and immediately become defensive.

So, many larger organizations build a cadre of internal facilitators of process analysis, in particular business analysts who often reside in their companies' IT departments. There are now also many experienced WorkOut, Kaizen, and Six Sigma practitioners out there in corporate Process Excellence teams; or, of course, they can be "rented" externally (shameless sales pitch!).

In summary, a neutral facilitator will:

+ Follow the agenda and the process
+ Manage time
+ Manage the interaction and discussion
+ Summarize, test for agreement, and press for decisions
+ Not get tangled up in the topic!

Decision Making

Group decision making can be very painful. All too often we have to deal with the trade-off of speed for support—see Figure 7-1.

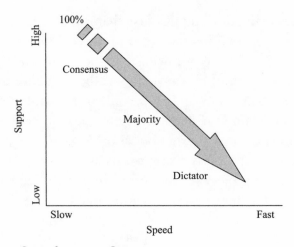

Figure 7-1   Speed versus Support

Of course, consensus, usually defined as "100 percent agreement to support the team's decision," is desirable, but it is rarely easy to attain due to time constraints. Dictators can make decisions quickly, but they don't find much support without a means of enforcement. Majority rule creates winners and losers, with the worst case leaving 49 percent still not in agreement. None of these methods is perfect.

Gaining consensus is generally most desirable and worth the effort. It takes time and careful attention to the discussion, the emotions in the room, and even the participants' body language. Key to acquiring consensus is facilitating an exploration of the definition of both *consensus* and *support* and agreeing upon how they will be confirmed. We've found in most cases that asking, with flip-chart marker in hand, "How would you describe consensus?" leads eventually to a definition of "we all can support it" in the end. This in turn makes it simple to ask, "What does 'support' mean?" We encourage discussing what appropriate behaviors look like too, often joking, "So, you mean that when we leave the room we won't say 'that sucked' or agree now and then withhold your resources later?" We remind folks that their behaviors later will be the best indicator of support:

+ Speaking positively about the decision, always
+ Delivering on the tasks and commitments necessary
+ Attending and participating in meetings

Key to Facilitation: Define *consensus* and *support.*

One of the best compliments I ever received was from an influential union representative participating on a project team I was facilitating. The team included managers, supervisors, and represented employees from two unions, so you can just imagine the challenging atmosphere: suspicion, historical issues and incidents dredged up, and hidden agendas on all sides. The union rep said to a constituent not on the team, in my presence, "For every bit of whining and posturing that goes on here, Roland has a hundred 'I don't give a s#!^s.'" This may sound a bit harsh, but the meetings and project have to stay focused on delivering results; and although entertaining, the stories and griping and recounting of old sins aren't productive. Don't interpret this as carte blanche to ignore the team members' perspectives or discount their dis-agreements—to the contrary, they need to be acknowledged and often addressed. But when they become patterns of behavior that threaten to disrupt progress, a firm but gentle hand is necessary. My mentor, Ord Elliott, used to remind me, "Don't forget when you're facilitating, you're really managing a project to deliver results—don't get distracted."

Key to Facilitation: Keep an eye on the goal.

As a final note to our discussion of facilitation, it's a lot easier to facilitate well if you've planned a strong agenda. Agendas are often misunderstood and much maligned beasts, and when they are too rigid and monitored too carefully, meetings become slave to them. But too loose or ignored, and the meetings become free-for-alls or don't deliver substance. With the right rigor, however, they include the key objectives, decisions, and deliverables, with adequate time allowances. Used appropriately, they are a road map for the time allotted, giving the facilitator time markers to test for agreement and to press for conclusion.

Key to Facilitation: Set a clear agenda.

Working Visually as a Team

If you've looked ahead, you know that one of the key steps to ETP is making the work and data visible in the newly designed process. We apply that same concept while working with the team throughout the project. Scribing the key points of a discussion, capturing conclusions and decisions in real time, and keeping ideas posted for reference are critical. This was made very clear to Roland during a project in one of the last years of the twentieth century. Companies were upgrading, rewriting, and swapping out systems that were at risk of a "Y2K" problem—failing to handle the date transition from 12/31/1999 to 1/1/2000.

I was facilitating an overly large team (24 people, if I recall correctly) chartered to reduce the complexity of the pricing structure of the breakfast cereals the company produced. It's unbelievable how complex cereal pricing can be! Folks were behaving pretty well, taking turns discussing an item while I scrawled out the key points on a flip-chart pad at the front of the room. Suddenly the previous speaker jumped up and shouted, "THAT'S NOT

WHAT I MEANT!!!" startling everyone. Silence. Then laughter, as people rewound in their minds what he had said while looking again at what I'd written on the flip chart: *exactly his words*!

"I know that's what I said, but what I meant was . . . ," he continued, amending his statement.

Had he not seen his words in large block letters on the flip chart, the assembled company would have continued the discussion from the words that came out of his mouth, not from his true intent. This was a powerful reinforcement to me of the value of accurately scribing the spoken words. There is much temptation to paraphrase, especially when the person speaking has rambled through three or four points, but paraphrasing transfers ownership of the scribed words from the speaker to the scribe. You can imagine that this is not a good thing . . . the trick is to ask people to paraphrase themselves, "Can you please give me the *Reader's Digest* version?" and then write their exact words.

Many times I've watched what I'll call "serial meeting participants" (project teams meeting in some sequential schedule) fumble unsuccessfully for some record of a decision made in a previous meeting, and other times I've watched them point and reference an old flip chart on the wall. If the team members are meeting in some kind of "war room" and are able to leave key flip charts posted from the first meeting to the last, they can have instant access to their past discussions. Physical or virtual, having a "homeroom" that can be used to keep the records readily available, public, and visual is an asset to project team performance.

Yellow Stickies

One of the best inventions ever for facilitation, as you probably know, is the Post-it note. By writing the participants' comments on "stickies" and then putting them on flip charts on the wall, the team can quickly organize and reorganize ideas visually.

Also, if you do have to change a comment, it's easy to tear one note off the wall and replace it with another one instead of rewriting a whole flip-chart page. After seeing some of our teams' work on walls of their war rooms, we often hear jokes like, "Do you guys have stock in 3M?" For the record, no, but we probably should get some kind of frequent-buyer awards from them!

By the time we met the folks at GPS, we were already well known for our use of yellow sticky notes, and the GPS folks brought a box of them to our first meeting. In our initial interview at the company years before, we were in competition with another consulting company that had its own software system to support change management. The competitors had presented their capabilities before our meeting, and so the evaluation team asked Dodd, "What software do *you* use?"

My answer, of course, was "Post-its!" and then an explanation of how teams need to work visually instead of electronically. We got the deal, and the rest is history!

Key to Facilitation: Keep the team's work visible using flip charts and yellow stickies on the wall.

Action Plans

Meetings become meetings for meeting's sake if they don't conclude with assignments to *do something*. All our project meetings conclude with action plans containing assignments of the action items for the next period. And all our meetings begin with a recap and accounting of the previous period's action items. Our format for action plans includes a description of the work and result, the "driver" (person accountable for ensuring completion), the "doer" (person who actually does the assignment), and the due date (a calendar date, not "one week"). This gives accountability to at least two individuals to ensure delivery and makes the expectation explicit. Woe to those who don't deliver.

The Cycle of Change

Change is an emotional adventure, a stream with rapids, calm, and eddies. Akin to the phases of "teaming" (forming, storming, norming, and performing), the change cycle is characterized as a circular series of phases of thought, emotion, and behavior that individuals work their way through when confronted with a change. Much has been written about the cycle of change, and several popular models can be readily found in books and on the Internet, so this is not intended to be a dissertation on the cycle; in fact we're going to suggest a rather simplified set of four phases that represent the essence of those available.

Our intent is to get you thinking about the impact of this cycle on your proposed change—what to expect, what to watch for, and how to manage it. Ignoring the effects of change on a person and an organization often leads to adverse outcomes: unhappy people, unproductive behaviors, even the departure of key players. We've seen situations where trusted, talented associates were assumed to be on board with the project while they were actually flying résumés that resulted in their escape. In their minds, moving to a new job was a less stressful change than sticking around to the end. (And unfortunately the best and brightest often have the most opportunities to leave.)

In many ways the cycle of change is quite similar to the grieving cycle that a person goes through when a loss occurs. People can deny it, fight it, run away, get stuck along the way, or manage their way gracefully through it. Each person will have his or her own pace through each phase, and everyone is at risk of getting hung up along the way or dropping into a posture of resistance. Some stakeholders can be allowed to stall in one phase, while others with more vital roles may need extra nurturing and encouragement to keep them moving along, and no one should be left a resister.

The phases, shown in Figure 7-2, include:

1. *Doubt, disbelief, denial.* Like the loss of a loved one, when a change is announced, the first responses can include doubt, disbelief, or even denial: "This isn't happening!" "Not here." "They can't mean it." Often a little bit of data can help people accept reality, and move along so they don't get stuck in this phase. It is, however, important to make a strong case to build that burning platform, and repeat it, repeat it, repeat it. We'll highlight a few more points and examples of building the initial case for change later when we discuss the eight-step ETP process.

2. *Acceptance.* Sooner or later (sooner, we hope), folks will move along to accepting the impending change and begin to speak in less doubtful terms: "*When* this happens..." They may still be resigned to their fate, but at least they don't

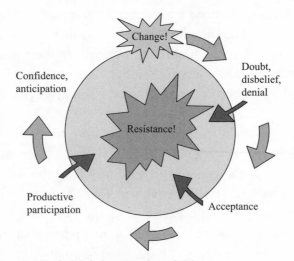

Figure 7-2 A Model of the Cycle of Change

doubt that changes are coming. Likely they begin to visualize what the future might look like, hopefully in a positive light. They can be helped along this journey by communicating and reinforcing a positive, realistic vision of both the path and the end of the rainbow. Inclusion, as we described previously, is also an important technique to assist them in their successful navigation through these phases.

Now, a critical juncture: although people can find their way into resistance at any time along the path, the transition out of acceptance is, for some, a fork in the road. We'd like them to move along to participating constructively in the process of designing the outcome, but some (especially curmudgeons!) begin to show signs of opposition, vociferously. "We'll wait them out." "It's just another 'program'; we've seen plenty pass through before." "This is stupid!"

Again, including them, even requiring their participation, will usually bring them along. Some will continue to squawk and disrupt meetings with their critical remarks, testing the patience of the facilitator and other team members; others will resist more passively by not showing up for meetings, not uttering a peep, blabbering negatively in the hallways, not finishing assignments, or withholding resources. These are all behaviors to watch for and manage, and are most quickly redirected by finding a way to engage the affected people in a positive role. Folks not on the core team can be engaged through outreach events such as informational meetings, focus groups for gathering data on specific topics, and subteams with carefully crafted assignments that will move the project along while giving them an opportunity to contribute, hopefully leading to a sense of ownership.

Some will try to bargain their way out rather than resist. They will seek ways to be excluded from either the project or the outcome, citing a litany of excuses. (Know the difference between a reason and an excuse? A reason is backed with fact; an excuse is a plea for mercy.) "My role is critical," "I need to stay with my group," "I can't afford the time," "What I do can't be changed," etc. Be prepared for it, armed with reasons, a vision, and encouragement. Critical roles need representation on the team, and they are often the most expensive resources to include, but their invested time is also likely to reap the most important productivity and cycle time gains.

3. *Productive participation.* Although many will still have doubts and concerns, we still have an opportunity or problem to solve, and we need to proceed with the project: measuring and analyzing, streamlining, making the work and data visible—all the steps of the ETP process. Moving rapidly into the measuring and analyzing phase will engage all the participants in learning new aspects of the work they do through gathering information and data about their process and viewing it through a different lens. Between the demands of their regular job and the needs of the project, they have little time for introspecting their way into trouble. A well-designed project plan rapidly executed keeps them off balance, making productivity on the project the easy path. Before they know it, the participants are telling their cohorts energetically how exciting the project is, recounting what important discoveries have occurred, and sharing glimpses of what the new world might hold.

It's always important to be wary of relapse though. Individuals, or sometimes occasionally most of the team, can relapse into worry that the future is not going to be so rosy and drop into resistance behaviors. If they think there is an alternate agenda, don't believe the data, or won't buy into the design principles, or if the rumor mill churns loudly enough, they can move quickly back to doubt and resistance. Listen to the hallway conversations and the anecdotes, watch body language and participation, and be prepared to act quickly to bring them around. As we've mentioned, involvement, communication, consensus seeking, and speed are techniques to prevent or reverse a relapse.

4. *Confidence, even anticipation.* Although not entirely necessary to proceed, helping team members and stakeholders gain confidence in their capability to create a new environment for themselves will accelerate the project. When they feel that they are "able to do it," develop a "will to do it," and even anticipate a positive outcome, the wheels roll more smoothly.

Confidence can be fostered by a successful demonstration, which is one of the important reasons for piloting a new design of the process and organization (not to mention piloting to test and prove the concept!). Occasionally with the members of a group that we perceive will be particularly difficult to win over, we will engage them in a simulation of a hypothetical, but similar, example—a structured "game" that first traps them in a "worst-nightmare" process and then guides them to a "Wow!" solution. This gives them a shared experience to relate to their real work and builds anticipation and confidence in their ability to create and implement a successful design.

Confidence and anticipation are also outcomes of a successful project— by living the experience, participants and stakeholders come out with a new faith in their abilities to survive, manage, and even drive change. These confident individuals can be ambassadors to other areas of the organization contemplating an ETP project or the nucleus of another team. The GPS production team is proud of its new environment and frequently hosts tours for leaders and associates contemplating or embarking on a similar journey.

Expecting and planning for these phases of response to a change is critical to a successful outcome, and helping all the members of the team transition gracefully is far easier than trying to drag them out of a resistant state or back from a relapse.

In the next chapter, we'll get back to technical detail and describe how to identify the right ways to measure the process to enable Engaged Team Performance.

Chapter Summary

✦ A best practice for driving performance improvement is to form a team consisting of both leaders and "producers" who do the actual work within the process.

✦ Strong group facilitation techniques help the project leader get optimal participation and input from all team members.

✦ It is important to include someone on the team who has the access and ability to query data from existing systems.

✦ Working visually in a project team room is far more effective than other methods, and the "war room" delivers a keenly focused perception to the entire organization of the critical value of the project team's work.

✦ Including people in the process and performance improvement journey results in better change acceptance from the entire organization.

✦ Anticipate and manage the phases of emotion and behavior that team members and stakeholders will move through (or relapse or get stuck in), the cycle of change.

CHAPTER

8

The Right Performance Metrics: Effectiveness and Efficiency

T HE MOST IMPORTANT measurements in a business process are those that drive customer satisfaction. On-time delivery of a defect-free product or service, with a smile, sounds so easy, doesn't it? So we start this chapter by reminding you that engaged teams only exist to serve a customer's need. All the measures and goals for performance of a team should somehow relate to the business's ability to efficiently and effectively meet the critical needs of its customers, and in this chapter we'll discuss the right ways to structure those measures.

As we said in Chapter 3, listening to the Voice of the Customer (VOC) is always a good idea no matter what kind of project or change effort you're pursuing. Customer focus is a key component of many prevailing business improvement approaches, including Lean Six Sigma. More recently, many companies have created customer loyalty programs to more formally listen to feedback, supported by systems and tools for market research and customer surveying. Cameron Karr, who led the global customer loyalty effort at Business Objects, says:

> *It's amazing to see how many executives make important strategic decisions based on urban legends—or worse yet—based on gut instincts. This is usually due to the fact that they need to make decisions quickly in the absence of good data. When they learn that we can gather customer feedback in weeks—not months—the conversation changes. And as a result, an increasing number of organizations are now staffing executive-level Advocacy departments to ensure the Voice of the Customer is represented in operational reviews on a regular basis. Executives can't spend their days talking with customers, so it's critical for us to bring the customer voice to them so they can make informed decisions on how to align the organization for growth.*

Measuring Effectiveness and Efficiency

Effectiveness is defined as a measurement of how well the process "does the right things right" for customers, while efficiency is a measurement of how many resources the process consumes in order to deliver that effective result. Until the process is able to deliver effectively for customers, it would seem to be a waste of time to worry about efficiency. Interestingly, the causes of both effectiveness and efficiency problems are sometimes intertwined.

The Group Proposal Services department had a number of customer-facing measures, particularly a customer satisfaction survey, a complaint tracking system, and a regularly reviewed turnaround time measure, which the department called TAT. In 2006, GPS had only existed for a couple of years, and the customer satisfaction scores had always been substantially less than desired.

Some of the reasons for that go back to the history of the organization. The GPS department was originally created after an expense analysis showed that quoting in the field offices was too costly. Most field offices were too small to generate the economy of scale to make the quoting process efficient because the variation in incoming requests resulted in the need to have enough labor available to handle the peaks. A centralized operation was certainly cheaper, but the new process resulted in some loss of control for the field offices; and so generally, there was still a feeling in some of the field offices that they could do their own quotes better and faster than the GPS department did, if they only had the time.

You may recall the Pareto chart with complaint counts from earlier (Figure 6-1). The top three categories of complaints from the field were all types of human error and accounted for 80 percent of the complaints. Until the project started, however, the team was making one of the classic mistakes in dealing with customer complaint data: it was responding to the complaints individually to fix the issues (right), but it was failing to look for trends in the overall complaint performance (wrong!).

As the GPS team members prepared their dashboard of measures for their teams to monitor performance, they added complaints and customer satisfaction ratings on time-ordered charts.

Though it might seem that 80 percent human error is primarily a "people problem," the performance actually got much better when the department implemented its process changes. Taking out three handoffs and having a single person complete each quote from start to finish helped to minimize the effects of misinterpretation, handwriting issues, and dispersed accountability. Complaint rates declined dramatically, and satisfaction improved. The department soon began to hear more compliments from field leaders.

The GPS department's annual customer satisfaction survey verified the substantial gains that the team had been hearing about anecdotally from the field sales team. Seven out of eight measures improved substantially from the 2006 survey, which was taken before the process changes, to the 2007 and 2008 surveys. Interestingly, the only measure to decline in 2007 was in the category "Frequent Communication"—the GPS leaders then realized that since the process had improved so much, the field team members no longer needed to call GPS to fix problems or ask "Where's my quote?" and were not interacting on the phone with GPS as often as they had in the past. So the GPS leaders implemented a proactive touch policy that brought that measure up significantly the following year as well!

Improving the turnaround time for quotes was a significant driver of the improved satisfaction too, of course, but it took a different kind of approach to fix. In reality, TAT was a measure of effectiveness that was *driven by efficiency*. A process with three handoffs takes longer to get the same work done because the item going through it (the quote) has to sit in three work queues for three different people. When you hear a person proudly state, "I work on everything I get within 24 hours of when I receive it," that sounds great until you realize that three of those people in a row would guarantee 2 to 3 days of waiting time to get a 30-minute quote done. That was exactly the challenge.

When the GPS project started, the department was measuring TAT as "percent of quotes completed within 48 hours of receipt." A good TAT was considered 95 percent, but the department rarely hit that goal, and during the busy season it had been more like 80 percent. At the end of the project, the department was measuring TAT in hours, looking at the typical (average) TAT as well as the variation (moving range). And after implementing the process changes, the vast majority of quotes were completed within 24 hours.

Efficiency is a measure of the "resources that the process consumes" to make the right things right (effectively!) for the customer. Measuring efficiency is often harder than measuring effectiveness, and almost everyone does it in a way that drives unintended consequences. Universally, the challenge seems to be separating the performance measurement from the *goals* that people like to set. They are not the same thing!

At the beginning of the GPS project, the department managers had a daily performance tracking system in place (good!) that was based on keeping counts of each person's "quotes done per day" (bad!). This was quite similar to some of the other individual measurement examples in previous chapters—at first glance, it seems to be the right way to measure things, but it drives the wrong behaviors. In this case, the magic number was 15.

Each person was expected to complete 15 quotes per day. The performance goal had been set based on observations of fully qualified specialists over the last couple of years, and in general it wasn't far from wrong. But the problems with the measurement became obvious once the team did some statistical analysis of the initial time study.

The analysis started with some simple internal benchmarking. There was one Sales Support Specialist (SSS) in the department whom the leaders singled out as by far the fastest quote generator. Instead of the expected 15 quotes per day, she was able to crank out an average of 18 per day. We went to see her first.

She seemed almost embarrassed about her greatness, and over and over she claimed that she wasn't doing anything special or different. She didn't mean to be faster than the other team members, and she was worried about all the attention. She couldn't identify any causes. Her manager said, "She's just a really hard worker." Perhaps she was even considering slowing down so that all the attention would go away.

But then we did a regression analysis of the time study information. Next, we'll explain this approach in detail, because it's a critical statistical tool to help drive Engaged Team Performance.

The GPS Mathematical Model for Standard Time

Basically, multiple regression is a statistical tool that allows you to analyze more than one variable at a time and see how the variables interact to drive an outcome. In the case of our time study, the department's leadership team had collected work time of specific quotes (the outcome), along with attribute information about each of those quotes. The quoting time was in minutes, and the team had brainstormed a few other factors that might make a quote take more or less time. You see, not all quotes are the same, and multiple regression analysis allowed the team to determine which attributes for a specific kind of quote drove the work time up or down.

To understand this, we'll need to explain a little more about group benefit quotes. Many companies, both small and large, have employee benefit plans, and those plans often offer health, dental, disability, vision, and life insurance coverage, for example. In order to quote the pricing for such a benefit plan, the broker or field sales office has to provide critical information from the potential customer (the "plan sponsor"). Some of the things that might vary from quote to quote were:

+ The number of employees to be covered by the plan (called "member lives")

+ Demographic data about each of those employees (ages, genders, etc.), sometimes delivered on enrollment forms and sometimes delivered as a summary in a spreadsheet (which is called a "census")

+ The type of work they do and how that varies in different company locations

+ The different benefit levels, deductibles, and options they'd like to quote (often driving the need to make different "versions" of the quote)

+ The quality and completeness of the incoming information, which might require additional data or further review by an underwriter

Without becoming an expert in quoting or getting overwhelmed by the details, you can see that it's a complex process. And while no two quotes are the same, you could probably expect that the variation in them would even out over time. It does.

And you'd also expect that every Sales Support Specialist would get a "fair draw" of incoming work to do. But on that you'd be wrong.

When we saw that the time study data had been collected as raw data with individual measurements of single quotes, rather than summarized counts, the department leader could see that I got pretty excited. Instead of having to collect new data, we were going to be able to quickly do a multiple regression analysis to see what factors drove the variation in quoting times. Ten minutes later (no kidding), we announced that the results were "spine tingling"—they had an equation that explained 75 percent of the variation in work time, based on a handful of critical factors. For a first shot at the data, that was pretty amazing.

Figure 8-1 shows the initial output. Without giving a statistics lesson in interpreting the output from the Minitab statistical software package, we'll briefly try to explain the significance of these results. With the p value below 0.001 and an R-Squared (adjusted) of 75.2 percent, we had found an equation with nine variables that explained more than 75 percent of the variation in total work time to make a quote.

That equation is at the top of the chart, and it expresses the total time in minutes to do a quote as the sum of the impacts of the different factors. While the mathematics and statistics required to *create* the equation would be hard to explain, the way we *use* the equation is really not too difficult: for each quote, the factors are replaced by the actual numbers that pertain to that particular piece of work

The regression equation is:

Total = 12.5 + 3.05 Versions + 0.249 Lives + 14.0 Multi-location + 16.9 LTD
        + 14.4 VTL - 6.71 Census Manipulation + 22.4 Benefit Choice
        + 14.9 Missing Info + 8.86 Underwriting

Predictor	Coef	SE Coef	T	P	VIF
Constant	12.544	2.429	5.16	0.000	
Versions	3.047	1.044	2.92	0.005	1.1
Lives	0.24877	0.05817	4.28	0.000	1.7
Multi-location	13.968	3.266	4.28	0.000	1.5
LTD	16.904	3.020	5.60	0.000	1.2
VTL	14.362	3.126	4.58	0.000	1.3
Census Manipulation	-6.711	2.453	-2.74	0.008	1.5
Benefit Choice	22.432	5.884	3.81	0.000	1.2
Missing Info	14.864	5.526	2.69	0.009	1.5
Underwriting	8.863	3.707	2.39	0.019	1.1

S = 8.956   R-Sq = 77.9%   R-Sq(adj) = 75.2%

Analysis of Variance

Source	DF	SS	MS	F	P
Regression	9	21170.7	2352.3	29.33	0.000

Figure 8-1   Regression Analysis: Total Time versus All Factors

(for example, perhaps one quote required "2 versions" for "12 lives") and then multiplied by the coefficients (the numbers to the left of each factor name). For the factors that are yes-no questions, you simply substitute 1 for yes and 0 for no and multiply that with the coefficients (yielding either the coefficient value or zero for each). Since not every quote will be exactly the same even when quotes have similar attributes, the calculated total time is just an estimate of the *predicted average* of a number of cases with similar attributes.

Figure 8-2 provides an example of a predicted work time for a specific quote, one that had 2 versions, 12 member lives,

The regression equation is:

Total = 12.5 + 3.05 Versions + 0.249 Lives + 14.0 Multi-location + 16.9 LTD
                + 14.4 VTL - 6.71 Census Manipulation + 22.4 Benefit Choice
                + 14.9 Missing Info + 8.86 Underwriting

Predictor	Coefficient	Value	Coefficient × Value
Constant	12.544	1	12.54
Versions	3.047	2	6.09
Lives	0.24877	12	2.99
Multi-location	13.968	0	0
LTD	16.904	1	16.90
VTL	14.362	0	0
Census Manip	-6.711	0	0
Benefit Choice	22.432	0	0
Missing Info	14.864	0	0
Underwriting	8.863	1	8.86

Total Prediction: 47.39 minutes

Figure 8-2   Regression Example

a long-term disability (LTD) product, and a need to coordinate with the underwriting department.

Looking at the coefficients intuitively, the equation made sense:

+ Each additional version of the quote added 3 minutes when additional versions were requested by the field office (often used for pricing comparisons).

+ For every four "lives" quoted, there was some minor data entry that added an additional minute (0.249 minute per additional employee covered).

+ But census manipulation, when it was available, using a spreadsheet to import personal data rather than manually entering it, *saved* 6.7 minutes (hence, the negative coefficient, which actually reduces the total work time).

+ Clients with multiple locations took an extra 14 minutes, and similarly quoting two complicated products (VTL and LTD) added about that much time too.

+ Requests with missing information and those requiring underwriting support (a handoff to another department) resulted in additional work time as well.

The equation was a major coup for the team. The regression analysis enabled the team to understand the variation in the work well enough to give fair credit for the inherent variation from quote to quote, which was a key factor in being able to predict the *standard work time* that each task should take.

As they progressed through the project, the team members were able to gather system data on the quotes that everyone in the department had completed in the last month and then run them through the calculation to determine how much "time credit" each person had earned. And—surprise, surprise!—the fastest person wasn't really the fastest! She was actually getting a slightly higher share of smaller and simpler quotes from the field office she supported. She was right that she wasn't doing anything different. In fact, she was exactly average. There were some other folks, however, who had been struggling to get their 15 quotes per day and were found to be doing more than their share of harder quotes. The equations even validated that there were times that a person could receive a "bad day" of particularly hard quotes, which explained why some people made their quota on some days and not others.

The team also verified that the variation in the time per quote drove some "easy days," where a person could hit the quota by the early afternoon. So the equation helped the leadership team see that setting a volume-based goal of 15 quotes per day was both unfair *and* unwise.

As the GPS department refined its work controls, it created charts to compare actual team performance (from self-reported task timing) with the standard time expected by the equation.

Basically, the department created a computer program to feed system information about completed quotes into a spreadsheet, which then applied the coefficients from the regression equation to predict the work time for each quote. A GPS systems analyst linked the spreadsheet to graphs that compared predicted work time for each quote with the actual reported time, with the ability to measure at both a team and an individual level.

The analyst started with the team chart in Figure 8-3 so that each team could compare its actual daily performance with the standard time expected by the equation. At an aggregate level, an equation's average predictions are quite accurate. You can see how close the team results matched the expected work time each day; this chart actually gave both the leaders and the teams great confidence that the process was being measured and predicted accurately. When the lines diverged as a trend for more than a few days, there was always an explainable cause; a new team member in training would cause a three- to four-week upward shift in the team's actual hours (higher than the standard time)

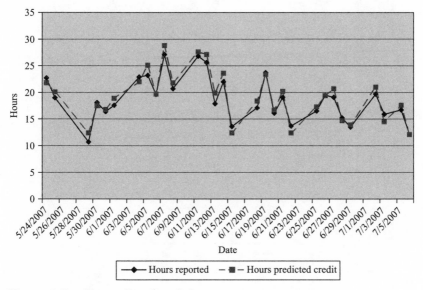

Figure 8-3   Team Productivity

until the person got comfortable with the product knowledge, process, and office preferences and began performing at a similar speed to that of the other team members.

Leaders and team members could clearly see how each team was performing.

As we discussed in previous chapters, measuring Engaged Team Performance always starts with measuring the *team*. But eventually, the leaders in the GPS department also created individual charts to share monthly with each team member. The variation in day-to-day quoting time was high enough that the individual charts weren't useful to judge daily individual performance, but they were quite accurate over the interval of a month to compare a person's actual work time with the standard. Figure 8-4 shows a recent example of an individual's monthly data.

Each person gets feedback on his or her predicted work completion credit, compared with self-reported time. In Figure 8-4, this SSS is right on her predicted time (the bottom two lines that almost match). The Hours Available (top line) measure is the amount of

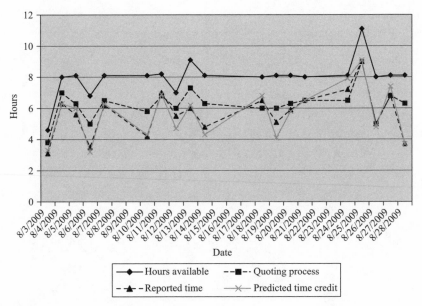

Figure 8-4   Individual Productivity

time that the person was paid to be in the building, while the Quoting Process time (second from the top line) allows comparison of time credit with the amount of time that the person was assigned to be doing production work. All in all, these measures let people know exactly how they are doing, and the end-of-year performance evaluation is never a surprise.

Best of all, because the predicted times match the actual times so closely in aggregate, the team members all have confidence that they are being measured fairly. Hard work can be recognized, and coasting is easy to identify. The team likes the measurements; people are OK with being measured when the measures are fair.

Hard to Measure Processes

How many times have you heard someone say, "You can't measure the performance efficiency in *this* department because every _____ (quote, widget, etc.) is different"?

As we have seen in the GPS example, every quote *is* different, but by gathering enough data about the factors that may drive the variation, and by using the right statistical tools, you can usually get a relevant estimate of the time it should take to do different types of tasks. Of course, some statistician somewhere is hopefully going across the room to pick up this book, having thrown it in disgust over a disagreement with our use of regression with both continuous and discrete variables at the same time, or wanting to see our residual plots or something. And to that, we'll just say, "Get over it. It works."

But we'd agree that sometimes it's just not possible to get an appropriate measurement of standard work time. An example of that challenge would be if we tried to create similar efficiency measures for a marketing department. Perhaps a marketing team is responsible for devising and executing three or four major advertising campaigns per year, and while the campaigns follow a similar process, each one really is different and there isn't a large enough sample of data from past campaigns to run it through a regression model. It would take years to wait for enough data to be collected.

So, as we said at the beginning of this chapter, efficiency is useless without effectiveness, and thus we'd suggest focusing there first. When we investigate further, the main outcomes of a marketing team's campaigns are probably supposed to be:

+ Awareness of the company's products in the minds of potential consumers

+ Interest or intent in trying the products in the near future (called a "trial")

+ Contact to a sales channel after seeing the campaign (called a "lead")

Of course, these actions are possible to measure only through an active-listening market research process that surveys prospective clients and provides feedback to the company. So instead of worrying about the efficiency, we'd suggest starting by designing a Voice of the Customer, market, and prospect feedback system to measure effectiveness. Web-enabled surveying software makes that approach to measuring market awareness and customer loyalty much easier and more effective today than it was in the past.

One such effort that we facilitated with a medical devices manufacturer found that 23 percent of the manufacturer's potential referring physicians had never heard of the product and procedure, and only 40 percent felt that they could explain it to a patient. It's hard to refer a patient for a procedure if you're not aware that it exists. The manufacturer's marketing team had some work to do.

When teams have an inherently hard-to-measure effectiveness outcome, measuring efficiency is often close to impossible. We frequently advise clients in those cases to measure the effectiveness first and see if they're getting the results they need. After that, they should try to make a relevant estimate of standard work time in order to gauge efficiency, but they should accept that it's simply an estimate.

If they can gather information over a longer period of time about the process, they can refine their estimate of the work time that a task (campaign, etc.) should take. They'll find that their initial estimate is often close to right. Usually, it's enough to keep the focus of the team on the key effectiveness results— remember: delivery of value to the customer is really the most important thing!

Another example of a hard-to-measure process occurred in a life insurance underwriting process, where a team had to produce departmental results for an upcoming Functional Review with the company's senior leadership team. In essence, the Functional Review was an opportunity to quickly study each business process in the company, collect effectiveness and efficiency data, identify opportunities to improve, and present the entire package as a 90-minute briefing from the department's director to the senior leadership team. The Functional Review was a great vehicle for senior management to drive accountability down to the departments. And the underwriting process is arguably one of the most important in a life insurance company; it generates the core evaluation of risk that drives pricing and long-term profitability.

The process of evaluating each life insurance application happens in small increments of time over the period of a number of weeks, which makes it hard to measure. The information often trickles in from the customer in pieces, causing the underwriter to have to touch the case multiple times. Anyway, in an initial discussion with a small team of underwriters, the team members estimated that the process took a couple of hours, and they used that estimate in the initial review and analysis. Later, after weeks of multivariable time studies that gave them greater insight into the process drivers, they adjusted the work time . . . to 128 minutes.

So the 120 minutes (2 hours) was not bad at all for an initial estimate, was it?

Sometimes close is close enough. As our friend and colleague Deirdre Gengenbach likes to say, "Roughly right is better than precisely wrong."

Staffing Models

For most processes, once the team has a reliable understanding of standard work time, the leaders can create a bottom-up staffing model. Of course, every leader in every business in the world already has a staffing model, but most of those are top down. That might not seem to be such a big deal, but it's actually a critical difference. Let us explain.

A top-down model is based on past history of a department's size and its volume. Often filled with multiple complex-looking calculations of volume mix, absenteeism assumptions, and performance adjustment factors, those models are inherently based on the assumption that if volume increases by 10 percent, staffing should increase by 10 percent. If anything screams "precisely wrong," it's the top-down staffing model!

The bottom-up staffing model starts from the work, calculating the number of people needed to crew the team based upon the volume of work, the standard work time, and certain assumptions of availability of people, based for instance on the amount of vacation that the company offers, the tenure of the team, and current attendance rates. Most of our models expect people to be working about five hours per paid eight-hour day. Reminds you of the magic equation that we introduced earlier, doesn't it? It's the same concept.

The GPS team actually calculated the work time and staffing numbers to support its new team concept using real historical volume data from the prior year. The team tried various configurations and combinations of field offices until it was able to divide the department into six equal-sized teams. It gathered system data about the attributes of actual quotes to feed into the regression equations, predicting the amount of work that each team would have needed to do each day, week, and month. It also looked at daily variation and designed the teams' sizes to handle the *average plus one standard deviation* of daily volume during the peak time period, with additional capacity for the rare heavy day to come from assistance from other teams or from overtime. Below is the final staffing model, which the team tested for both typical and peak expected volumes:

Team	1	2	3	4	5	6
Average work time/day (Aug–Mar)	838	1,103	1,421	1,022	1,476	1,307
Standard deviation/day	288	284	438	358	488	405
Recent Volumes						
Average work time/day (Feb–Mar)	907	1,132	1,559	1,047	1,514	1,361
Standard deviation/day	249	233	337	293	415	357
AVG + 1 STDEV =	1,156	1,364	1,897	1,340	1,929	1,718
Staffing at 5-hour days (FTE)	3.9	4.5	6.3	4.5	6.4	5.7
Recommended staffing:	5	5	6	5	7	6
Peak 2005 Volumes						
Average work time/day (Sep–Nov 2005)	895	1,121	1,503	1,113	1,652	1,433
Standard deviation/day	301	243	425	366	463	395
AVG + 1 STDEV =	1,196	1,365	1,928	1,479	2,116	1,828
Staffing at 5-hour days (FTE)	4.0	4.5	6.4	4.9	7.1	6.1
Recommended staffing	5	5	7	6	7	6

The numbers showed that Team 3 would need an additional person during the busy season, which could come from the training department since training would be curtailed during those three months. The team had a great plan!

At the time, nobody believed that the department could do the work with only 36 people (the bottom row of the chart shows the final team sizes, which add up to 36). In the first busy season after the project was implemented, the department actually had quite a few more people than that available. Over time, through teamwork and performance management, the department gained confidence that this staffing model was actually right. Two years later, after attrition of employees who weren't replaced, the department was down to 38 people, including leadership and support.

Mark Reynolds, the director of customer experience with Equinix, recalls from his tenure with Interwoven the way that data helped to engage the team. "Provide actionable metrics—data—then keep them engaged in the process. Success is watching them play it out."

We said earlier that Engaged Team Performance can't work without data, and hopefully this chapter has allowed us to demonstrate what strong control measures look like. What you measure gets done. And if you measure it right, you can get it done right! Then you just have to get the team *engaged*.

Chapter Summary

+ Effectiveness means delivering what the customers need, when they need it, and how they need to receive it. It is ultimately measured in customer satisfaction, but it can translate into revenue growth rates.

+ Efficiency is a measure of the internal resources that are required to deliver effectively for customers. It is often measured financially in cost per unit produced, but for transactional processes, it's often just as easy to measure efficiency in "work time per unit" produced.

+ Work-time studies are analyzed with advanced statistical tools like multiple regression to determine the *standard time* that certain tasks (and variants of those tasks) should take to complete.

+ Functional Reviews and staffing models use volume and work-time data to calculate individual, team, and department efficiency rates and predict the number of team members needed to effectively serve customer needs.

Team Goals

Iₙ 25 yₑₐᵣₛ of coaching youth soccer, a coach gets to experience both the joy of watching children learning to play the game and the pain of dealing with the annoying behaviors of their parents. One particularly memorable season, a mother was paying her son to score goals. Her child was quite talented, and he was able upon occasion to dribble through an entire defense and score. Unfortunately, he was also willing to shoot from *anywhere*, and the rest of our team quickly learned that he was never going to pass the ball. In time, his teammates stopped getting in position to receive passes, and the entire offense was abysmal any time he was in the game, except for his occasional highlight-reel goal.

We eventually had to explain to the boy that he would come out of the game every time he shot the ball when the coaches determined that he should have passed. Shortly thereafter, one such incident resulted in an argument on the sidelines, with the boy remaining on the bench for the rest of the game. The mother filed a formal complaint with the league.

The only thing worse than having no metrics would be creating the wrong metrics. Measurements drive behaviors, and bad measurements drive bad behaviors.

With every soccer team in the 10 years since then, we've begun the season by standing in the corner of the 18-yard penalty box, with the team huddled and staring toward the goal. The coach says, "I made the best play of my life from this spot on the field, back when I was in college. Anyone want to guess what happened?"

"You scored a goal?" one kid always asks. It would have been a heck of a shot from that spot on the field.

"It was the semifinal game of a 36-team league tournament at our college, and we were tied 0–0 with the best team in the league. I had a breakaway run and brought the ball down to this spot, and the goalkeeper came over to cut off my shot. I had two defenders closing in on me from the side and another behind me ... Without even looking, I kicked a light pass across the field, trusting my teammates to know to go to the right spot. I never saw the rest of the play, because I got knocked down making the pass. One of my teammates, Sue Kelley, calmly shot the ball right into the goal. And do you know what our team did after that? They all came out to congratulate *both* of us, not just the shooter. My best friend Sam Cochrane came all the way out onto the field to pat me on the back. And I'm going to do the same thing with you on this team; in fact, I will always first congratulate the person who made the assist and then later the person who made the goal. An assist is the most important play you can make on this team this year."

True story. And to this day, the assist maker on our team gets the first recognition.

By the way, hockey teams keep track of "points" in individual statistics for both an assist and a goal. They're equally weighted. Hockey also has another great individual measurement called "plus-minus" that really measures individuals based on a team outcome—all players get a point when their team scores while they're on the ice, whether or not they contributed to the goal. Likewise, all players on the ice lose a point from their plus-minus tally when the opposing team scores. This measurement tells people whether good things or bad things happen when you're on the ice, and over the long term it's a very effective gauge of an individual's contribution to the team result.

Ultimately, whether you're running a soccer team or a business, the only goals that really count are team goals. As we'll demonstrate throughout this chapter, you can't get Engaged Team Performance without team goals. ETP relies on teamwork and collaboration to drive efficient and effective performance, and as we explained in Chapter 4, individual goals just drive individual behaviors that may not fully align with the team's intended results.

The Right Goal—A Refinery Story

In the sweltering summer heat of Louisiana about 10 years ago, Roland was being escorted on a tour of the operations and maintenance areas of a large oil refinery; and "sweltering" is no understatement—100 degrees Fahrenheit, 100 percent humidity, and then we walked past an operating unit shimmering with even more heat! This refinery had been around since the 1960s, through various owners, upgrades, hurricanes, and floods; and due to its location among tiny river communities, employees were often related or connected outside the plant. Brothers worked alongside their sisters, with fathers and uncles on duty or recently retired. Folks saw one another buying groceries, or going to church, or coaching, watching, or playing sports. Although there were probably some "Hatfield-McCoy" disputes, they weren't obvious, and everyone seemed to know one another and get along.

We were charged with guiding a transition from a traditional multilevel hierarchical organization to something leaner, more efficient, flatter, and more focused on the process. You can probably imagine the challenges we were facing! There were several bargaining units, multiple shifts supporting 24/7/365 operation, and personnel that were pretty well entrenched in their way of doing things. Our plan was to implement ETP by drawing on the tools of the Sociotechnical Systems and Lean Six Sigma methodologies to provide structure for escorting the plant personnel through this adventure. Managing the change process was foremost in our minds.

Refinery operation is pretty basic:

1. If the stuff is in the pipes or tanks, you're probably OK.

2. If it is on the ground or in the air, something is very wrong.

3. What goes in must come out (if not, refer to #2).

On our first day, it seemed that the plant was operating normally—nothing was spilling on the ground, there was no flare, and the people were quiet, efficient, and typically curious about these consultants tromping around their domain. The plant manager had graciously given us an overview of the site from a map and photographs and even given us the view from a hallway. Now we were in tow, going from unit to unit, alternately suffering in the heat or chilling in an air-conditioned control room. Each unit performs a specific task, for example converting Arabian crude into intermediates ranging from solid coke to tar to oils, fuels, lubricants, and fuel gases; and all are interconnected with pipes, valves, and tanks. It was an impressive tour.

Standing quietly, listening to the lead operator describe the function of the Crude Unit, out of the corner of my eye, I noticed a wild swing occur on a graph displayed beside me. Our host ceased his presentation and jumped to a seat at the control console, and together the two operators kept the stuff inside the pipes.

"Ah, teamwork!" I thought as we watched them dance among the switches, dials, displays and gauges, almost choreographed!

"What just happened?" I inquired.

"Downstream had an upset . . . we'll have to dump to a tank for a while, then reprocess. We won't make quota," he snarled.

Sensing from his tone of voice that all was not right, I observed, "Does this happen often; could they warn you?" Remember, they're connected firmly together with pipes, and the folks in the different units very likely go home together in the same pickup truck.

"Yeah, they've probably been working on it for a couple of hours now," he responded.

More discussion uncovered that their process need not have upset and caused re-refining (and failure to meet quota!), had they been given even 15 minutes notice by their downstream "partners." My associate and I exchanged knowing looks. "We're on to something here," we were thinking.

Each shift on each unit had a production goal, measured in total barrels per shift. Unit efficiency and utilization, operator performance and maintenance effectiveness, all were keyed to this goal, which was watched like a hawk. Process tweaks were made across shift changes to maximize unit output, frequently when the downstream process couldn't accept the product.

The plant had an overall daily production target that was frequently unmet and excused with a litany of reasons. Three shifts on more than half a dozen units meant a lot of goals and reasons for failure. Today's reason had just occurred.

Obviously the plant needed to be a team, with collective responsibility to produce the plant goal. Not so obvious was how to get from here to there. We'll tell the rest of the story in later chapters as we walk through the ETP steps in more detail.

Productivity Is *Not* a Goal!

Productivity is an *outcome*, not an individual or even a team goal; and treating productivity as a *goal* can have, you guessed it, negative unintended consequences.

We once led a process streamlining effort for a team that did outgoing calls at prearranged appointment times with customers. As in most call centers, the telephone system allowed the managers to monitor the call activity quite closely; and while they enforced typical schedule adherence measures, they still found through benchmarking that their call center was not as efficient as other comparable operations.

So the management team had initially set individual goals for productivity. Each person was expected to complete a certain number of outgoing calls by appointment per day.

You won't be surprised to hear that the goals didn't work. Actually, you've probably already guessed that the goals were hurting rather than helping the process.

The cause was rather interesting, though. Sometimes customers weren't available for their appointments when the call center representative called. The operation was always staffed just for the right number of appointments, of course; and so when a representative called and got no answer, that employee was left with nothing to do for 30 minutes until her next scheduled appointment window. It was very frustrating for the employees, knowing they were accountable for productivity and being unable to force a customer to pick up the phone.

Again unsurprisingly, another bizarre behavior began to sprout up. The team leader began to be called in to referee arguments between team members about "working ahead"! It seemed that some team members realized that if they called a little early for their next appointment and didn't reach a customer, they could quickly go to call the next customer on the list, effectively "stealing a call" from a coworker. It was like a game of musical chairs. The team was forced to adopt norms with peer pressure to prevent the practice, and sometimes people violated the social contract with their peers when they were not meeting their individual productivity goals.

After we found out that the customers' missed appointment rate was a consistent 33 percent, the answer was quite simple:

relax the time windows that customers commit to be available, and "overbook" the appointments like hotels and airlines do. Team productivity improved, and there were no more fights about stealing work. There was plenty of work to do.

This story illustrates a key concept about productivity. Productivity is a product of the management team's ability to do two things:

1. Get team members to contribute a fair amount of work in a day.
2. Size the team appropriately for the amount of work that needs to be done.

A team that is right-sized and appropriately managed, employing all the Engaged Team Performance concepts we've discussed, will have an opportunity to be productive. A team that is undersized for the amount of work will be hyperproductive until the team members burn out or the customers abandon them. But a team that's oversized for the amount of work will be invisibly unproductive. If there aren't enough calls to make, the call center representatives can't possibly meet an appropriate productivity standard, and it's not their fault at all. But rather than complaining about not having enough work to do, most team members will try to *find* something to do. Unfortunately, the activities they find are not always valuable for the customer and the business.

We sometimes call this effect the "room in your garage" problem. If you don't park your car in your garage, that empty space seems to attract stuff. A small pile of necessary things starts to attract other things, and soon your whole garage is filled with junk. We had a yard sale last year that earned just enough money for us to hire a trash company to come and get the rest of the stuff. It actually felt good to break even on that deal.

Contrary to the old theories of Scientific Management, managers don't need to manage people. Numbers don't manage people either. Managers just need to *use* the numbers—particularly volume and standard work time—to figure out how to deploy the right people to the right place at the right time. When that's done right, *the work can manage the people*, and people can manage to get all the work done to meet the team's goal, which should be related only to meeting the customer's needs. The manager's job is to size the team accordingly, monitor the numbers, develop people, and stay out of the way.

Productivity should not be a goal. Productivity should be the outcome of a well-designed and well-run process. Perhaps it's an obvious point, but if the team is sized right, the team's goals can and should be very simple:

+ Get all the work done.

+ Meet all the customers' needs.

+ Win the game.

Team Goals and Productivity in GPS

As we saw in previous chapters, some of the variation in individual results in the GPS department was caused by differences in the quotes themselves, not the performance of the people. But the individual goal was still 15 quotes per day—and everyone thought the goal was right, even though it wasn't delivering much value in motivating anyone.

As we proceeded with the GPS project, we found that the time to make a quote was a function of a number of things, and we demonstrated statistically that 75 percent of the variation in work time was driven by concrete factors such as versions, products, and lives. Therefore, individual effort was worth at most 25 percent (and probably a lot less).

We also explained in a previous chapter that the concept of *tomorrow's work* came from a behavior that the GPS team members adopted to ensure that they always met the individual goals. Again, the logic was something like:

- ✦ Something that arrives today is not "due" until two days from now.

- ✦ As a Sales Support Specialist, I have to do 15 quotes per day (my goal).

- ✦ Due to the inherent variation in incoming volume, I'm not sure how many quotes will come in tomorrow from the field office I support (sometimes it's even zero!).

- ✦ Since I only usually do work for this one field office, I have to save 15 of its quotes to do tomorrow, or I will definitely fail to make my goal tomorrow.

- ✦ Therefore, anything that comes in today is tomorrow's work, and I'm probably also going to stop today (or find something else to do) after I finish 15 quotes, so that I can make sure that I have enough to do tomorrow.

The project team confirmed the impact of the goal on individual behaviors by monitoring the process directly for a few days and observing that people who had met their daily goal by the early afternoon would often stop doing quotes and start working on other tasks (training, special projects, answering e-mails, etc.). As we suspected, not only was the 15-per-day goal failing to drive productivity; it was actually *reducing* productivity!

The individual goal distracted the people from the real team goal, which, of course, should have been to *get perfect quotes back to every customer on time.* Because defect-free quotes with a smile are nonnegotiable (those results should still be measured, of course, but the goal is perfection), the turnaround time was really the only team measurement that needed to be treated as a goal. But it needed to be a *team* goal, not an individual one, particularly because of the variation in incoming volume. Sometimes a team member didn't have enough work from his or her assigned field office and really should have done some of the quotes from another team member's office. But that didn't happen because there was a perception that it was too hard to learn another office's preferences. Ultimately, with individuals only accountable to deliver a certain number of quotes per day, the only person whose goals were really tied to the customer's experience was the manager, and that's a very bad deal for the manager.

So the GPS team created a simple goal for the teams: *get all quotes back to the customer, done right, within 24 hours of arrival.* Each team measured those results—turnaround time in hours, with quality scores—on a white dry-erase board, along with trend charts with other predictors (also called "leading indicators") such as incoming volumes, current work-in-process inventories, and cross-training status. Teams that were within goal timing were constantly recognized, and small incentives such as pizza parties were occasionally awarded as well. These incentives were team incentives, of course, with all team members sharing in the recognition for meeting the team goals.

The GPS team also used a team incentive of "blue jeans weeks" for teams that were going through the extra work to pilot the new process. Suspending the company's dress code policies for teams that were performing to expectations during the pilot phase turned out to be the most motivating team reward. The employees appreciated the relaxed environment as they were learning new processes and trying to reduce cycle-time results for the customers. It was a win-win; the incentive didn't cost the company anything, and the employees valued it.

Before they implemented ETP, the members of the team really hadn't been acting like a team. They were just a group of people supervised by the same manager. A team works together. These folks just worked in the same location as individuals, just like Team USA in the 2004 Olympics. In order to achieve Engaged Team Performance, the entire GPS department first needed to come together behind a team goal. Next came the harder work of making the measures and goals visual, and then integrating and aligning them with new processes, organization, and collaborative norms, all of which we'll discuss in the next chapter.

Chapter Summary

+ While individual goals sometimes create problems, team goals can drive great results.

+ Efficiency and productivity do not need to have goals! If the management team uses the appropriate data to create a proper staffing model, the team will be sized "just right" to be productive.

+ Team goals should be simple, often relating to meeting key customer needs. Occam's razor says that the simplest solution is usually the best. Straightforward team goals are the key to Engaged Team Performance.

The Fluid Organization of the Future: Making the Transformation to ETP

D RIVING ENGAGED TEAM Performance first and foremost means that you have to form a team. It has to act like a team. It has to be measured as a team.

Then the team has to learn to work together. It has to care about the outcomes that it creates for its customers. It has to adopt the processes, norms, and standard practices that support efficient and effective ways of collaborating. It has to acquire and sustain the necessary skills and knowledge for its human resources. It needs a new kind of leadership, where the leader provides the information and guidance that the team needs in order to allow every person to continually make the right decisions to support the team's goals.

Visual Control

One of our children started first grade recently, and her new teacher has a very effective tool to allow the children to regulate their own behavior. Mounted on the wall is a large stoplight, which continuously shines a green, yellow, or red light. The stoplight is attached to a decibel monitor, and as the noise level in the room gets higher, the light changes colors. The children understand the negative consequences of a red light, and the device gives them a chance to monitor and adjust their own noise level before the teacher has to intervene and administer discipline. Some of the children will even point at the light to influence their classmates to tone it down. What a great idea!

In the GPS department, just like any other successful team, part of the transformation involved changing the process, and part of it required a change in measurements. One of the key challenges of driving Engaged Team Performance is that the process and measurements are highly interdependent, and so a change in one necessitates a change in both. Thus, as we deployed both sets of changes, the GPS team had to redesign its work area to facilitate the integration of the new processes and measurements.

As we've already illustrated, the most important team goal in the GPS department was the one about getting all the work done for the customer, regardless of which individual on the team did it. To assist the team in *seeing* that performance, the leaders made some changes to the work area to enable *visual control*. Visual control is a key concept of Lean Enterprise that encourages work-flow, status, and problems to be visually obvious. Anyone who walks into the work area should be able to ascertain how well the team is doing just by looking around. The concept is not as hard to apply as it sounds; it sometimes just takes some "first grade" creativity!

Prior to the improvement project at GPS, each Sales Support Specialist (SSS) kept the requests for quotes on an electronic list, composed of e-mails in an Outlook folder. Every day, each SSS would print a batch of requests (usually 15!) and keep the stack of papers on his or her desk. If there were leftover requests at night, those would be locked up since they had privacy-controlled data on them. The work was hidden in desks and computers, with no way to see how much was there. Every morning, the team leader would hold a meeting to ask if anyone needed help, and each SSS would update a whiteboard with count data about the inventory of requests, sorted by age in days. The leader and the team would have a similar recap near the middle of the day to recalibrate, again trying to shift resources if needed. Like a stopped clock, the numbers were right twice per day! All the rest of the time, nobody really knew how the team was doing overall in meeting the customers' turnaround time requirements.

To change the team's perception of the timeliness goal and increase its awareness of performance, the pilot team first changed its seating arrangement. Rather than having desks in cubicles in separate rows, the pilot team moved to an open "cell" structure, with all team members' cubicle walls lowered and the desks facing inward toward the team's center so that the members of the team could communicate and collaborate. The whiteboard with the performance data went onto a table in the middle, as did a new tool: a stack of trays. Instead of hiding the work in and around individuals' desks, the new process required the quote requests to reside in trays, one three-tray set for each field office, with the top tray for rush orders (due today) and the two trays below that for quotes due on the following days. At any moment, any team member could look at the trays and identify how well the whole team was doing. From the location and thickness of the stacks of paper, everyone could see which offices needed immediate support in order to meet the team's goal. Every night, the work in the bottom trays was moved up one tray higher, and the process started again the next day. The work was now visible.

The team also needed the *data* to be visible. During the pilot of the new process, the team had to briefly create a new role to control the workflow and reporting system. One volunteer, who turned out to be a great contributor and peer leader for the department, became a "simulated computer program" to manually gather information and display it for the team. Her main role was to count the work-in-process inventory in each bin every two hours and post the updated information on the whiteboard. She also printed the quote requests, put them in the trays, and counted all the work as it was completed. It was a tough job for her because she would have preferred to spend all her time doing "real" work, but the team needed to measure the performance in order to understand the process capacity. Later, after the process design was validated and the team was comfortable with the setup, most of those tasks were automated by the information technology group, with status reports that could be printed on demand. The lesson for the team was that sometimes the benefits of visual control and measurement are worth a little bit of extra-yet-temporary work.

Another client had a similar experience with the powerful effects of simply changing the layout of a team's work area. David Cline, vice president of regional operations for Harland Clarke, says, "The biggest surprise that we discovered when we piloted our first work cell was the natural teaming that occurred. We have taken pride in being a strong team, and it took creating a cell layout to see a true team in action helping across all process steps. The barriers to great teamwork turned out to be our departmental thinking and equipment layout. We discovered that without a great cell layout the full benefits of teamwork cannot be captured."

Out of Sight, Out of Mind

After the GPS team piloted and implemented the process, the department received a challenge from some of the leaders who toured the new GPS work areas. The leaders noticed the paper quotes in the work trays and commented that we'd taken a step backward in the company's twenty-first-century drive to become paperless. Dismayed, the team members explained that the paper actually helped them see the work. A paperless process could be achievable, but they believed that the team needed to learn first how to be efficient with paper. (As an aside, the GPS team very successfully went paperless in 2008.)

This is going to sound like heresy to some of you . . . as it did to those leaders back then: *paperless is not automatically better.*

We started another project with a client recently, and the client's reason for launching the project was that its new paperless system (image and workflow, with a new automated system feed) had reduced its capacity and extended its cycle times. After some analysis, we found that the new high-tech tools added at least 25 percent more work time to the process compared with the time it took using the old manual way. Even worse, the up-front imaging process had two steps—"image" and "index"—with their associated handoffs, each proudly accomplished within 24 hours . . . resulting in 1.5 days of average cycle time before the production associate even first touched the work.

Also, the workflow system had great new capabilities to "suspend" and "wake up" work, allowing task requests to be touched, attempted, put down, and then brought up later to "follow up" (sometimes unsuccessfully). Any task that an associate couldn't figure out how to do could be transferred to the in-box of another associate, and a task with missing information could be put away in the system with a "wake-up date" to attempt again later. We have a name for that type of technology: "bad habit enabling."

When we asked why the client made the changes to go to the new system, we heard something like, "We had to make the changes in order to ensure data integrity as we migrated to other new systems. Our company is going paperless. We didn't do the project to focus on being more efficient; it was something we had to do in order to link our systems."

Sometimes a paperless system makes sense, and sometimes it doesn't. In this case, it *did* make sense, but it had been implemented inefficiently. The project managers had simply assumed that paperless was better, and they hadn't thought about finding ways to prevent handoffs and keep the work and status visual—the latter being a key characteristic of ETP. After a few process changes, some new measures, and a little bit of self-discipline in handling only the work that was ready to be done, the process was back up to speed.

Collaborative Norms

Engaged Team Performance might seem to encourage individuality and free expression within the definition of "engagement" of people, and to a certain extent, that freedom is essential to gaining buy-in from the team members—but it actually also requires more self-discipline once the team establishes its norms.

Ord Elliott makes this argument in his book *The Future Is Fluid Form* as well: while a fluid organization might seem less disciplined, it's really less *supervised*, which means it really requires more *self*-discipline! The team must set up processes and practices that support the team's goals of satisfying the customer.

Collaborative norms are really just tactical-level processes, but they're so detailed that many companies don't document them. They are the ways that people work together. To get to Engaged Team Performance, the right collaborative norms need to be established, documented, measured, and maintained. Though they're executed at the individual team-member level, it's very important that the team members buy in to them and enforce them among themselves as a group. Most important, the collaborative norms and the team goal have to be mutually supportive; the entire team has to feel passionate about performance.

As we've discussed in prior chapters, the key norm that needed to change in GPS was the sharing of work. Before the reorganization, each team member was assigned to work with a single field office, usually doing only that office's quotes and rarely helping anyone else. The people believed that it was too hard to learn another field office's preferences, and so there was a perceived artificial barrier to collaboration. Unfortunately, the inherent daily variation in incoming work would guarantee that a person would be too busy one day and not busy enough the next. Instead of sharing part of a task by "prepping" for someone else—which entailed a handoff, dispersed accountability, and didn't really work anyway—the team members needed to learn to support each other by doing whole quotes for other field offices that weren't their assigned ones. The department decided to create six teams, per the staffing model in a previous chapter, and established norms around the following principles:

+ Each five- to seven-person team was cross-trained such that two or three people could know the benefit preferences for each sales office that the team covered. Everyone didn't know the details for every field office, but enough people knew enough of the office details to be able to level the workflow across the team on a day when one office sent too many quote requests and another didn't send enough, or when a certain team member was out on vacation. Each team made a matrix to track its cross-training status.

+ Within each team, there was no more talk of "my office" and "your office"—all the customer offices supported by the team became "our offices," and team members were expected to pull the next request either by priority or by "first in, first out" from the trays that were located in the center of their area. Team members also took daily turns printing as requests came in, not printing all as a batch at the beginning of the day.

+ Rather than pulling up a day's worth of work in the morning, each associate was now expected to pull quotes from the team's work inventory bin in priority order *one at a time*. This allowed the entire team to see how much work was still available and from which offices. Before the process changes, a team leader had to move work between people when needed, but soon the team was able to do that on its own. A key realization was that the new work distribution method got rid of the concept of "yours and mine" so that all the work became "our work"!

+ Before the changes, the people were measured on their individual output (quotes per day). After the changes, the *team* was measured on how many quotes were *left* at the end of the day, with the intention to sustain an ending number less than the team's daily production volume (i.e., get the process cycle time under 24 hours so that something that arrives today gets done by tomorrow). Creating intolerance for backlog is sometimes the hardest part of the mindset to change.

+ The manager of the area also committed to an action item to approach field offices that were sending quote requests in batches and ask that they send each request immediately as it was received from the broker to smooth out the incoming flow of work.

The last item in the list is worth a moment of special consideration here. In addition to using data to manage themselves, engaged teams can also start to use that data to manage their suppliers and customers better. Instead of simply reacting to others' priorities, collecting data about incoming work can, for example, allow the team to become more proactive about coordinating workflow issues with its customers, driving more value for both.

As the GPS teams began to accept the new vision (perfect quotes delivered 30 minutes after receipt) and the new team goal (reducing cycle time to under 24 hours), they found that the collaborative norms supported the metrics and the team goal because everyone was focused on the same thing. The visual controls told the team members what work needed to happen, and they collaborated to make decisions on the fly about which work tray each of them would pull a request from next. The team was beginning to become engaged!

Transforming to a Fluid Organization

Although many associates were kept in the same team(s) or were supporting the same offices, there were some people who had to learn new office preferences, and then the teams needed to accomplish the cross-training plan before the busy season hit. The GPS team was able to plan to phase the team changes and training over the summer months. The cross-training turned out to be a lot of work, and each team had to be adequately trained before it could make the jump to the work-sharing norms that were required.

This was reorganization the right way: the reorganization of the work, process, and metrics led to a planned, purposeful, and well-timed reorganization of the team—ETP in its essence. Anyone who has survived a reorganization taking the opposite approach will recognize the difference. The wrong way to reorganize starts with a secret meeting to discuss "who's going to lead what group" and eventually ends in a brief discussion of "what does each group do." In contrast, the GPS reorganization was actually remembered by the team members as a tough experience with a very positive outcome! We were able to interview a panel of GPS team members at a training event the following year, and they confirmed that it was hard work to make the changes, but they'd never want to go back to the way the process and the organization were before.

The department leaders initially ran and then occasionally updated a staffing analysis for each team, using the regression model to predict the amount of work time using actual quote volumes (both from a recent time period and from the previous busy season). They then recalculated the necessary staffing levels and adjusted the team composition and office assignments accordingly. This staffing model precisely balanced capacity and demand for each team. The analysis was done monthly during the transition, and then the department reassessed it quarterly to ensure that each team maintained the proper resources and capacity to meet its current and future expected demand.

The cycle time came down and the work efficiency came up as the changes took hold. As turnover happened on the teams, unfilled positions were not replaced if they were no longer needed. Eventually, the teams were working at their true capacity.

The field offices started to notice the change in performance effectiveness quickly. The vice president of field operations, Jenifer Moses, says, "The company had made changes to GPS before, but we had always changed standards and volume mix instead of changing the way we did the work. After this change, we immediately noticed a dramatic improvement in timing. The real 'tell' was when some of the most vocal field sales reps started using the GPS to do more of their quotes."

Cindy Close, one of Jenifer's team members, adds, "There was a change in timing, of course, but the difference in quality was just as important to us as the timing." And that feedback was based on reductions in complaints and cycle time; the field offices didn't know at the time that the transformation also came with a labor cost savings of $1.2 million per year as well. Cindy says, "At some companies, the field might see a home office cost reduction as a possible indicator of reduced service levels, but this was the opposite. Costs and service both improved. It was a win-win."

Sustaining Skills and Knowledge

One of the metrics that the department decided to formally track in the future was the cross-training status. Knowing that the ability to share work was critical to team performance, the GPS team created a matrix for the individual teams so that each team could keep track of which team members were trained on which office preferences. The matrix was placed on the whiteboard with the other metrics. The teams also set a standard for refresher training, forcing cross-trained team members to occasionally pull some quotes from each of the field offices that they could support, so that they didn't lose their capability.

The teams' assigned office lists were organized by region and by "complexity": there were two teams of "high-complexity" offices, two teams with "lower-complexity" offices, and two teams that covered offices that needed a slightly different process for doing quotes. This reorganization of the teams enabled a different development path, where new team members would be on-boarded to the two low-complexity teams and more experienced associates could move up to a higher-complexity team as their product knowledge grew.

Whole books have been written on skills assessment and job design, and we won't repeat that content here. Candidly, we often find that some of those books can encourage people to overthink the roles, skills assessment, and job design before they challenge the process, metrics, and norms. But obviously, we agree that once you decide what's important to know and do, the leadership team needs to provide appropriate opportunities for associates to develop, *track*, and sustain the requisite skills and knowledge.

Leading the Engaged Team

Leading Engaged Team Performance is different.

In 2008, we had the great fortune to bring another team that was starting a new performance transformation project on a tour of the GPS area. Coincidentally, one of the former leaders of the new project's department had recently been transferred to GPS and was our tour guide. So, all the leaders in the new project's department knew her and trusted her, and she knew the challenges that they faced because she used to work with all of them. After hearing her enthusiastic description of the process and the metrics during the tour, one of them asked her a great question: "So, what's different about your job now?"

Initially, she scared them by saying, "Well, you might think this is a bad thing, but I spend a half hour every morning to make sure the metrics are posted and the team sees them. We have a team huddle to discuss the current status, yesterday's performance, and any special situations."

Heads nodded. One person commented, "Yeah, we'd never have the extra time to do that data work." Just for a moment, I was worried.

But then the tour guide–leader said, "And after that, I don't have to do anything special to make sure the work gets done. I don't have to check to make sure people are working. I don't have to move resources around. I don't have to babysit anything or anybody. The team takes care of the work. You know me, and I know what you have to deal with in your department, because I used to work with you. The difference is that I spend a half hour on the metrics and then I get to be proactive all day. I get to spend the day doing my job, interacting with our customers, and developing people." Wow!

The key to completing the transformation to Engaged Team Performance lies in completely *integrating* processes, measures, team goals, visual work, collaborative norms, and organization. It's hard work both for leaders and for their teams, and sometimes it can take months or even years to accomplish. After leading the transition, leaders need to provide the ongoing coaching to sustain the team's skills, monitor the work, and continue to improve both process and performance. The leader's job in an ETP team becomes a lot more fun.

Chapter Summary

+ Teams have to learn to work together.

+ Visual control allows work, measures, status, and performance to be visually obvious to the entire team in the work area. Paperless systems (e.g., image and workflow) require special attention to deliver timely and useful performance data to the team.

+ Collaborative norms are ways that team members can share or shift work in order to meet team goals.

+ The transition to ETP can sometimes take a lot of work and time, as people cross-train to learn new skills that allow collaboration.

+ Sustaining ETP requires a new kind of proactive leadership, focused on maintaining and improving processes, listening to customers, and developing team members.

Expectations, Rewards, and the Motivation to Excel

UNDERSTANDING GENERATIONAL DIFFERENCES and the ways that people of different ages interact in the workforce can be critical when tailoring the Engaged Team Performance approach for a specific company, team, or situation. We'll investigate the generations for a few minutes and then look at the factors that really influence success as a member of an engaged team.

The Generations

Many, many words have already been written about the various generations and their divergent and complex needs, and different analysts have even categorized the generations differently. For example in *Growing Up Digital*, Don Tapscott identifies the Net Generation, which he proposes begins with the tail of Gen X and

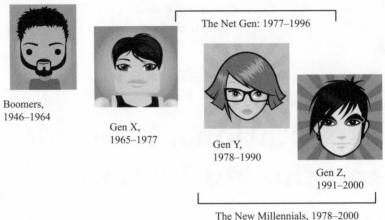

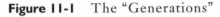

Figure 11-1 The "Generations"

spans Gen Y into Gen Z, while Cam Marston in his book *Motivating the "What's In It For Me" Workforce* proposes that the New Millennials encompass Gen Y and Gen Z. Regardless of the source, the one key theme might seem to be that the young people just joining the workforce are generally unemployable. In all seriousness, there are some significant challenges to overcome when managing different generations. Let's look at each generation individually.

First, there is the now-retiring Baby Boomer population—born of the recently returned World War II veterans in the late 1940s and early 1950s. Many were shaped by the 1960s' culture—the Vietnam War, protests, peace, drugs, and free love; a few moved to Key West or Santa Cruz to drop out and became surfboard carving entrepreneurs, and a few more are leaders in today's businesses but don't remember (or won't acknowledge) their activities during their younger years. Most of the Boomers only participated vicariously in the frolic of the 1960s through music and television, yet they are the core of the knowledge base, experience, and management today. Geography, circumstance, upbringing, and social position contributed either to a healthy skepticism of the "Establishment" or to a willingness to conform. Certain communities (Berkeley, Haight-Ashbury, East Village), many college campuses, draft eligibility, education, and parental control (or lack thereof or revolt against) shaped these individuals.

The Boomers typically began their careers during their parents' reign (these parents are referred to as "Matures," born between 1909 and 1945, by Cam Marston in *Motivating the "What's In It For Me?" Workforce*). Coming from a time of high employment and a tacit "social contract" with their union or employer that they could, with adequate performance, expect to work their way to a nice retirement, the Matures discovered later in their working lives the meaning of "at-will" employment. Some companies couldn't continue to compete, some cut costs to survive, and some were absorbed; all resulted in a changed world for employees. No longer could they expect to work through retirement for one company. It became apparent that even building a retirement fund was the responsibility of the employee, and the regulations were eventually changed to encourage portability.

Boomers, of which Roland is one, at first didn't believe it, then were forced to confront the reality. My dad, after many years of public service and nearing retirement, lost his job with a city government due to consolidation of departments resulting from Proposition 13 (the "taxpayer's revolt" of 1978 in California). He was crushed. I was scared. I'd heard about the capriciousness of employers, but this was a municipality! (After a period of astonishment, he moved on and had a very fulfilling second chapter to his life.) Shortly after this, I left a small family-owned company that I probably could have worked with to retirement (my ex-boss's children run it now) and joined a Silicon Valley manufacturer of floppy disks (remember those?).

Growth, expansion, hiring, advancement, success. Until there was a glut of floppies and the advent of the "shirt-pocket" 3½-inch diskettes.

The company struggled, and then abruptly we were bought by a competitor; the handwriting was on the wall, and bam! I'm on the street. Not a big surprise; I had seen it coming and was flying résumés, but it reinforced my desire for industry and market knowledge that could be used to manage my career. How different from my father's generation.

Boomers had two reactions to this loss of social contract with their employers: they grumbled and began to watch their environment for signs of trouble, and they felt that they themselves were no longer restricted from making decisions that caused others to lose their jobs.

Boomers. They are what they are. The key takeaways are that they are a product of their individual environments, they witnessed and lived through the demise of any social contract with employers (and started to "pass along the pain"), and they are largely in positions of control today. And like most parents, they are skeptical of the performance and capabilities of the younger workforce.

Next in line are dubbed the Gen Xers—also labeled the "baby bust" generation, due to the unusually low birth rate compared with that of the Boomers. Gen Xers were raised in Reaganomics and the politics of George H. W. Bush, their births coincided with the release of the horror movie *Rosemary's Baby*, and they grew up with the fall of the Berlin Wall. Joining the workforce as loyalty to and from a company was in a full rout, they became generally free agents and developed a mind to direct their own careers. "Layoff, whatever . . . ," they say. With technology on the beginning of its meteoric rise, the Gen X kids accept and use the electronics available to them (we even offer that they should be called the "bug generation"—as a result of their experiences with a fledgling industry; their tolerance for cranky, awkward, and error-prone devices and software is high). "Whatever, I'll buy the latest one," they say. The older Gen Xers are the beginning of the tech-savvy workforce.

Up next, Gen Yers: as Bruce Tulgan describes them in *Not Everyone Gets a Trophy: How to Manage Generation Y*, "Generation Y is Generation X on-fast-forward-with-self-esteem-on-steroids." Growing up with the reality predicted by Moore's law (which states that the power of microprocessors would double every 18 months without corresponding increases in costs) and raised by parents in an environment where no one is a loser, they characteristically are confident and self-possessed. Aptly referred to as the Trophy Generation (when they played soccer as kids, score wasn't kept, both teams won, and everyone got trophies), they are tech-dependent information junkies who communicate globally, impersonally, instantly, electronically. Indulged by ready access to information and by their parents, they want context and acknowledgment. Not satisfied to just manage the changes in their careers, they feel entitled to specify workplace conditions and job requirements. Roland's son, Barrett, recently visited his first job fair seeking an internship, and thinking forward to graduating from the university and getting a "real" job, he lamented, "Why can't they pay us a little less and only expect 30 or 35 hours per week so we have time for surfing and dirt-bikes?"

Tulgan identifies a subgroup of the New Millennials as Gen Z: born since 1990, the oldest ones will be finally able to legally buy a beer soon. Just graduating from high school, or early in college, they won't begin joining the workforce for a while, but watch out! In addition to all the attributes of Gen Y, their middle schools, high schools, and colleges have set them up to work on projects in teams and to build PowerPoint presentations and deliver them confidently; they are convinced they could (and should!) be presenting to the board of directors.

The Motivators to "Do the Job" or to Excel at Work

Money, power, status, winning: these are the more overt drivers of behaviors at work; we've all seen them. Unfortunately, it's sometimes very effective to step on toes and faces to move higher in the hierarchy and earn more. For some people, it's all about where they sit, how much they make, what they drive, and how many people work for them. These are more difficult behaviors to channel for success in an ETP environment—a little is good, but too much may lead to trouble. Some selection of candidates based on these characteristics is in order, and you should be prepared for some to "opt out" after experiencing the ETP environment, or you may see some "voted off the island" by the team.

Community is more important to an ETP environment. Engaged Team Performance leverages the desire to work with people that could be considered friends, in the comfort of a "community" at work, with shared objectives. It creates a community through common goals, self regulation, colocation, and careful selection of team members.

Everyone has seen the clip of Lucy and Ethel on their first day in the chocolate factory—the conveyor belt running ever faster, the women unable to keep up, cramming chocolates in their hats, blouses, mouths . . . (*I Love Lucy*, episode 39). A frustrating situation made hilarious! But that situation is not so funny in real life. It wasn't in the days of Henry Ford's assembly plants, nor is it now; in a remarkably high percentage of today's jobs as shown on Science Channel's *How It's Made*, the teams have little control and are unable to keep up with the production line. The results are both failure and a feeling of being dehumanized until a robot replacement can be programmed. This feels like the sad workplace that Adam Smith envisioned centuries ago!

Jobs that allow the producer greater degrees of team member control garner higher satisfaction ratings—reference the basic principles of Sociotechnical Systems in Chapter 2: more autonomy and whole, meaningful tasks with closure delivered better results. As we proceed into the implementation steps for Engaged Team Performance, you'll see these principles behind the work processes and organizational designs.

Another aspect of the control motivator is participation in the design and operation of the reward system, accomplished in ETP through the team's participation in designing the processes and organization—don't be tempted to leave the team out!

The youngsters of today have an astounding need for context. In an earlier time, we might have referred to them as the "big-picture thinkers"—the folks that routinely step back for the global view. "How does this fit in?" they are asking themselves. The New Millennials and particularly the Trophy Generation subset, probably partly from their access to information and partly due their upbringing and education, want context. Roland finds himself frequently frustrated with the monster we've created—his 20-year-old son, Barrett:

> "Could you go to the store and get some pickles, Barrett?"
>
> "Why?"
>
> "We're out."
>
> "Why now?"
>
> "We have guests coming over for lunch."
>
> "What are the pickles for?"
>
> "JUST GO GET THEM!" I want to shout.

He wants the whole story, so he can decide for himself if it is relevant and important enough to do (no matter that he was just watching Travis Pastrana jump motorcycles on Nitro Circus MTV for the fourteenth time). The first step of the ETP transformation process establishes the context and seeds the team's actions with the big picture, and it's important to recognize that some people need to understand that picture more than others.

And last, but not least, is the "cool factor"; although Google's trajectory makes it seem possible, not everybody can work at Google. As the dot-coms gained momentum, and some gazillionaires were made in Silicon Valley, the cachet associated with a person's place of employment has risen in importance to (occasionally) surpass salaries. More recently, this has translated to other industries, and now everybody at the University of Vermont wants to work at Burton and design, build, or market snowboards and gear (oh, and not come to work on a good snow day . . .). How do you compete with that?

Today's Challenge

These entertaining generational paradigms tell only part of the story, points out Trish Martin, vice president of customer service with CyberSource—there is certainly a component of the "nurture" of the nature-nurture debate in addition to the natural generational attributes of each person. Factor in parental involvement in their lives, add their schooling and educational experience, and mix liberally with their many natural attributes, and you'll find all patterns in all the generations.

"Everyone wants to have a purpose," says Joe Austin, vice president of customer experience with Juniper Networks, "perhaps simply to have the money to enjoy life away from work and to have an identity within the organization." This "identity" is also what makes it difficult for people to change their environment or employer. The announcement of a coming change threatens their communal identity, while structuring to increase this sense of community makes it "stickier" and easier to retain people. ETP teams develop a strong identity through their shared goals and constant interaction.

Just as the Trophy Generation wants context, developing a team, and particularly integrating a team based on a common sense of community, requires that the candidates and the team get to understand each other. Folks being considered for joining the team, without regard for their generation, should interview with the team; the team should share its norms and team identity (treat the interviewees like Trophy kids); and the team should have final say.

"On-boarding" of new team members may require some coaching of the existing team, depending on the team's diversity of generations—and a discussion of the various generational characteristics with the team in preparation for negotiating the flow of a new member's integration can be priceless. Reminding an old dog like Roland of the perspectives and nuances of accommodating the likes of his son can make the transition of a Trophy Generation associate into an ETP team smoother.

How do you build a highly motivated team that will continue to be yet more productive without making the team members feel like they're being squeezed, especially as we move through periods of tough economic conditions without the ability to add staff? Look forward to Chapter 13, Steps 5 (*organize the team*) and 6 (*set team goals*), for the fundamentals of establishing teams that manage themselves to meet the customer's needs while taking individual accountability for supporting team goals.

While accommodations can and should be made to meet the needs of the various generational characteristics, it will be a subset of each cohort that will be successful in an ETP environment: those with a desire for community, self-governance, group recognition, and delivery of results for the customer will succeed there, just as the individuals with tremendous drive are uniquely suited to thrive in the pressure cooker at GE. Managing through the journey with each person on the team will mean respecting the team members' different perspectives and motivators and ultimately creating an environment that will both respect them and benefit from them going forward.

Trish Martin says to "remember that it's a workplace; it's a job—what is important are the behaviors that need to be consistent with the workplace and the work to be done. Honesty, integrity, the ability to look you in the eye, to give consistent answers, to be part of a team, to overcome challenges in life, all are important. Yeah, some want to be the CEO next week, some are living in their cars, and some have a sense of entitlement, but you have to connect to the things that are important for each person, and those things are different for each generation."

Ultimately, you have to just "drive behavior—the numbers lag the behaviors," says Scott Bajtos, senior vice president with VMware.

Chapter Summary

✦ Teams are composed of people, and people are all different.

✦ The different generations are a product of their unique experiences. The generations are easily stereotyped, and the individuals within them do share some common attributes.

✦ Some people will find the ETP team environment undesirable, due not so much to their generational characteristics but to their individual attributes. Selection for the right characteristics will build a team that will thrive.

✦ Have the team share its community with candidates during the interview process, and give the team the authority to make the final selection.

✦ Discuss the generational differences with the team during on-boarding of a new member.

✦ Drive behaviors; it's a workplace; it's a job, not a country club.

CHAPTER

12

The New Age of Collaboration: New Paradigms in Organization and Competition

T HINKING ON A larger scale than the departmental work team for a moment, we recognize that Engaged Team Performance may be making its way into other, informal, collaborative human organizations. As mentioned, Ord Elliott calls this idea "Fluid Form" organization, and the concept can apply to moving resources across organizations, harnessing collaboration between separate groups, or even driving global efforts to improve the world where we all live.

We've already presented some of the tactical implications of the ideas from Ord's foundational book, *The Future Is Fluid Form*, but his vision is even more valuable as a new strategic way to structure organizations in the future. Supporting the competitive need for greater flexibility and speed, and capitalizing on the individual needs for self-direction and reduced hierarchy (particularly the Gen Xers and Gen Yers), he describes an organization that is truly process and project oriented with fewer functional groups and fewer vertical stovepipes.

Characterized by an environment where decision making and coordination are performed by networks of key stakeholders instead of command and control, Fluid Form organizations are flatter with fewer functional or department heads. Since decisions are made by networks of people that have a stake in the outcome, expertise in the operation and what the results should be, and know-how to get these things done, they don't need the hierarchy. Boundaries disintegrate, leaving fewer interfaces that have to be managed. He envisions a more collaborative executive suite, more of a leadership council focused on coordination than a pyramid of oversight and control.

> *Ultimately, in Fluid Form, you have the right people in the right place at the right time—people with a stake in the outcome of a given project or process, a broader sense of expertise than they would have had if they had remained isolated in their cubbyholes, and ownership of the endeavor. Because they're becoming decision-makers, they are growing as leaders. They're better equipped to decide for themselves if they're on the right track, if something should be stopped, if energy should be re-directed, if a plan should be reformulated, or if a process should be repopulated with individuals possessing a different set of skills.*

Work becomes much like going to school, with different classes and courses and with the individuals developing broader experience. There isn't the same pressure to specialize since success is built on what you do, who you are, and what your talents are, not where you sit on the org chart. "As the networks grow more successful and people come to rely on them," Ord notes, "they see those networks as better ways of managing initiatives, projects, and processes." The projects, processes, and initiatives are more self-managing under Fluid Form.

While Ord has taken a more strategic view of a flat, flexible organization and the steps to evolve into it, Engaged Team Performance is the tactical path to transforming a smaller team—a division, a department, or a production group—through focus on both the process and the people to drive a rapid quantum leap in performance.

First a few words on some of the recent discoveries coming from that "great disruptor"—the Internet.

Free-Form Internet Collaboration

You may have noticed a few references in this book to content that is available on Wikipedia. You probably know that Wikipedia is a free encyclopedia on the Internet, with links to popular Internet search engines.

Similar to the disruptive effects of open source software like the Linux computer operating system, Wikipedia is breaking the business model that information should cost money, instead harnessing the power of free human collaboration to generate, review, and approve content. Think of it as the equivalent of the "ask the audience" help line in a popular TV game show; it's not always perfectly right, but it's usually much more knowledgeable than the person asking the question. So while it is not always the most trusted of media sources, Wikipedia has the advantage of being very easy to use, it is quickly updated and amended if incorrect (the word *wiki* derives from Hawaiian for "quick"), and it draws upon the collective wisdom of a vast number of contributors.

Everyone Wants to Contribute

Referred to as a "peer production" environment, Wikipedia integrates the talents of dispersed individuals. What drives those individuals to contribute to Wikipedia? Several personal and social incentives have been identified: pride of creation; exposure; peer acknowledgment; fame or notoriety; and altruism to a social goal (solving world hunger, saving the rain forests, and building a free encyclopedia, to name a few).

Enablers of peer production include sincerity and trust, especially trust in the benevolence of that particular endeavor's operator (prediction: watch how fast Wikipedia comes unraveled if Jimmy Wales puts advertisements on the site for his sole profit!).

Making It into a Game

Creating metadata or tags has proved to be a task beyond the capabilities of computers (for now!), and well suited to humans, if you can get them to do it. Google Image Labeler is a feature of Google Image Search, in the form of a game that allows the user to label random images to help improve the quality of Google's image search results. Originally developed as the ESP Game by Luis von Ahn of Carnegie Mellon University and licensed to Google in 2006, Google Image Labeler is a game in which two people simultaneously view an image with no way to communicate other than learning that the other person matched their label for the picture or seeing the pass signal. Names from two contributors that match become the keywords for future users searching the image, while each contributor racks up points based on a value assigned to that name. Since the only thing the partners have in common is that they both see the same image, they must enter reasonable labels to have any chance of agreeing on one. More specific names like "Roland Cavanagh" get more points than "Author." It is said that some people spend

40 hours per week online competing in this game. Google profits by getting human-tagged images, and contributors collect virtual points, have a sense of belonging, and get satisfaction from having contributed.

Now Mr. von Ahn has a Web site using a form of the ESP Game to determine the most beautiful pictures, music, etc., all in the name of making computers more intelligent. As you play the games, you are teaching computers things that they don't know yet (Game with a Purpose, www.gwap.com/gwap). Irrelevant tidbit: an interesting variation is reCAPTCHA, which takes advantage of the collective 150,000 hours per day that people spend responding to Web site security measures while improving the process of digitizing books. It sends words from scanned books that cannot be read by computers to the Web in the form of CAPTCHAs for humans to decipher, CAPTCHAs being the squiggly words that are presented as a security measure to prevent bots from gaining access to protected information.

Coase's Law, Backward

Coase's law, loosely translated, states that an organization will tend to expand until the cost of the next transaction within becomes equal to carrying out that same transaction on the open market. Originally presented by (now) Nobel Laureate in Economic Science Ronald Coase in his paper "The Nature of the Firm" in 1937, the law was derived from a macrolevel analysis of the economies of scale of the emerging large corporations such as Ford Motor Company and U.S. Steel. "If the marketplace is the best mechanism for matching supply with demand, why don't individual workers act as individual buyers and sellers?" Coase asked. He posited that in complex environments like manufacturing a car, the costs associated with negotiating individual transactions between workers exceed the costs of control in a hierarchical organization. Tapscott and Williams in *Wikinomics*, discussing the effects of the Internet on today's businesses, suggest, "The Internet has caused transaction costs to plunge so steeply that it has become much more useful to read Coase's Law, in effect, backward: nowadays firms should shrink until the cost of performing a transaction internally no longer exceeds the cost of performing it externally. Transaction costs still exist, but now they're often more onerous in corporations than in the marketplace."

In our microenvironment of an ETP team, we're removing many of the interpersonal- and interprocess-step transactions, with their associated handoff and delay costs; and through skills alignment, colocation, and team goals, we are rendering the ETP team far more efficient and effective than a set of distributed functions under central control. In some cases, implementation of an effective ETP team has forestalled outsourcing transactional production processes to foreign countries.

Self-Monitoring

Another old concept that has become the subject of much discussion is the Panoptic Model of Surveillance. In 1785, English philosopher and social theorist Jeremy Bentham proposed a novel design of a prison based on the plan for a military school that his brother conceived. The concept of his design is to allow an observer to watch all prisoners without the prisoners being able to tell whether they are being watched, creating as Bentham himself described "a new mode of obtaining power of mind over mind, in a quantity hitherto without example." Basically since they don't know if they are being watched, they behave. Comparisons have been made between Bentham's penology model and Frederick Winslow Taylor's introduction of Scientific Management into the factory, where surveillance is key to control. New technologies have expanded surveillance in the workplace with e-mail and phone call monitoring and closed-circuit security cameras.

The current discussion centers on the gathering and commoditization of personal and behavioral information by Internet ad servers like Bluestreak and DoubleClick so that advertising and marketing firms can serve up materials targeted to individual consumers, increasing the probability of a purchase.

Any way you slice it, surveillance costs money, time, and effort. There's a price to pay for the technology, time, and effort for someone to view the content that was captured. Consumer information appears to have sufficient value to justify the expense, trading technology costs for reduced distribution costs of marketing materials and ads. But surveillance in the workplace is simply a non-value-added cost, offset by the myth that people will "do the right thing" if watched, or at least if someone else becomes an example by getting caught misbehaving.

Self-surveillance is the ultimate "power of mind over mind," and is intrinsic to most individuals if they are given adequate instructions and feedback on their performance. The only costs associated with self-monitoring are that of logging and displaying key data to the producer—no supervisor looking over the shoulder, no technology "spies" or locks to prevent shopping on eBay. ETP builds in the fundamentals for self-surveillance with clear process instructions describing the work to be done and with immediate "scorekeeping"—feedback to the individual and the team of their performance against their metrics.

Group Norms

Ori Brafman and Rod Beckstrom in *The Starfish and the Spider* talk about "Circles"—one of the five legs of the decentralized organization they embody in their spider.

> *Circles . . . depend on norms. Alcoholics Anonymous has norms about confidentiality and support. Wikipedia has norms for editing entries. The Apache software has norms for developing code. Burning Man*

*has norms for maintaining a gift economy . . . Because they real-
ize that if they don't enforce the norms no one will, members enforce
the norms with one another. In doing so, members begin to own and
embrace the norms as their own. As a result of this self-enforcement,
norms can be even more powerful than rules. Rules are someone else's
idea of what you should do. If you break a rule, just don't get caught
and you'll be okay. But with norms, it's about what you as a member
have signed up for, and what you've created.*

Embracing norms engenders trust among the team members,
creating a desire in all to play fair and to support one another,
as well as support the norms. Our ETP teams begin developing
norms and building trust during the data gathering, analysis, and
design of their new process and organization—that's why we
emphasize including them, nay, *requiring* their participation, in
the project. These project norms and trust carry over into the
new production environment, contributing to success.

Chapter Summary

+ Fluid Form establishes the vision and path to a flatter and
  more flexible organization, whereas this book looks at steps
  to propel a division, department, or production group to
  new heights of efficiency and effectiveness.

+ Several motivators have been discovered or become more
  pronounced as the Internet has matured: collaboration, the
  desire to contribute and belong to a community, productive games, and group norms. All are components of the
  ETP structure and organization, quietly capitalizing on
  their benefits to drive results.

+ ETP, like the Internet, decimates the costs of information
  transfer.

Deploying Engaged Team Performance within Your Organization

Eight Steps to Deploying Engaged Team Performance in Your Organization

I<small>N THIS CHAPTER</small>, we'll delve deeper into the Engaged Team Performance methodology and discuss how to apply the eight steps to achieving ETP within your organization.

The GPS story in the previous chapters provided a comprehensive vehicle for explaining both the value of Engaged Team Performance and the overall approach to achieving it. Below, we'll briefly summarize that approach so that anyone considering implementing ETP can use it as a guide; then, throughout the rest of the chapter, we'll give direction on implementation.

Figure 13-1 is a tactical overview of the key aspects of ETP. Obviously, there are lots of factors to consider, and all organizations

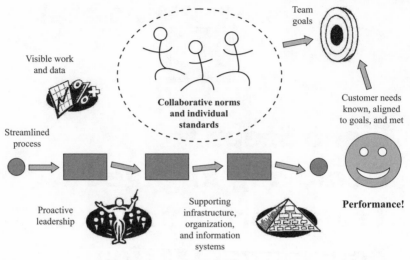

Figure 13-1 An Overview of ETP

and processes are different, but the basic principles and steps are the same everywhere:

1. *Commit to change.* Articulate a burning platform for change.
2. *Measure and analyze the process.* Investigate the current process and customer requirements, and measure outcomes and work standards.
3. *Streamline the work.* Improve the flow of the process to deliver value efficiently.
4. *Make the work and data visible.* Make the new work processes, collaborative norms, and control measures visually obvious in the workplace.
5. *Organize the team.* Reorganize and right-size the team for the work.
6. *Set team goals.* Assess team performance and establish team goals.

7. *Lead the transition.* Make a rational plan, and develop the skills, tools, systems, and knowledge to move the team to the envisioned future state.

8. *Sustain Engaged Team Performance.* Demonstrate performance over time!

As we recap the approach, we'll illustrate the steps with the story about an oil refinery that successfully implemented ETP.

Step 1. Commit to Change

If you've read this book up to this point and are not just joining us here and now, you probably already understand the value of Engaged Team Performance and likely even see some potential benefits of applying it in your own organization. But sadly, even the promise of a 20 to 50 percent efficiency gain and the potential growth impact from vast improvements in effectiveness and customer satisfaction are not a guarantee of commitment.

We always hear people say they need to "build a burning platform" for change. One memorable leader at a beer distributor used Management by Objective (MBO) to drive and stretch his teams' performance, but his junior leaders laughingly called it Management by *Emergency* (MB*E*) behind his back, since he was always trying to manufacture a crisis so that he could sweep in and solve the problem. It soon became tiresome for his leadership team. It's an unfortunate reality that burning platforms are hard to *build* over and over. They present themselves all the time; you need to identify and broadcast them. They have to be real. And often, they have to be personal.

That brings us to the refinery project that Roland launched in 1999, which we introduced in Chapter 9. At the time we didn't even know we were doing ETP; we just knew that it worked!

As a standard business practice, refineries are partially paid for their services with an allocation of a percentage of the price of a gallon or a barrel of product. As such, when the price of oil is up, they make good money; when it is down, they struggle to break even. January and February 1999 saw oil at a 15-year record low of $9 a barrel, with no apparent end in sight. Refining was not a good business to be in. To reduce capacity, sections of plants were shut down for maintenance, and the less efficient refineries were being considered for temporary shutdown or retirement. The burning platform was obvious: to keep one's job the plant needed to stay operating; to keep running it needed to produce at a lower cost per barrel than others. Easy to articulate, this provided the incentive and vision to mobilize everyone "inside the fence" to tender everyone's support.

In the GPS story, every person on the team, from the associates doing the quoting to the senior leadership, had just survived a horrible busy season in late 2005. As we began that project, every person on the team was committed to trying *anything* that would drive a better experience in the future. The burning platform was staring us in the face.

But imagine if the busy season hadn't been so painful. What if the company had just "staffed up" the team to be able to handle the volume even with its previously inefficient processes, metrics, goals, and norms? Actually, when they're operating with top-down staffing models that are based primarily on managing volume changes, that's exactly what most companies do: they resize the group to handle the new volume, whether up or down, and they never realize how inefficient they are. When that happens, the only people who have a burning platform are the shareholders, but they don't know it.

The department leaders in an inefficient business should have a burning platform too, right? Maybe. In an environment where leaders believe that they're accountable for the long-term performance of the process, or where those leaders see personal benefits in being an agent of change, perhaps that's true. Being involved in driving ETP for their teams has certainly delivered personal benefits for many of the leaders we know.

But many department-level leaders are more cautious. In essence, their biggest fear is that they'll cut too deeply and then have a performance crash if the work volume changes. Ultimately, being inefficient is bad, but failing to deliver the required production volume, which results in backlogs and back orders, is much worse. So leaders tend to use that age-old behavior that props up inefficient processes: *sandbagging.*

The term comes from a number of card games like spades and bridge, where the game forces players to commit to a number of "tricks" that they can take. The incentives promote risk aversion by penalizing a low estimate lightly but causing significant damage when a team fails to achieve the committed number, even by a small difference of one trick.

You can see the business parallels: a leader may be chastised if she's caught carrying more resources than she needs, but the consequences are much more dire for her if the department ever fails to meet a key customer need. So, it's easy to see why department leaders want to hold back a few extra resources, just in case an unexpected situation comes up. They usually don't know exactly how much extra they have, but they're terrified of finding out (by reaching the minimum threshold!). Consequently, the departmental leader's risk aversion is often a significant obstacle to change.

Senior leaders, of course, want to ensure that their departments are adequately resourced to deliver the right results too. As we've already discussed, they often try to get continuous performance improvements each year by asking for a "stretch" improvement in efficiency. This behavior actually contributes to the sandbagging effect, because the departmental leaders are forced to hold back some resources so that they'll have some to give up on demand. It's a self-perpetuating fallacy.

One solution to all this is the Functional Review that we will describe in greater detail in Chapter 14. By setting up a *routine process for leaders to regularly assess and report* a set of standard effectiveness and efficiency measures, the senior team can make informed decisions about resources and investment in change opportunities. Without an obviously burning platform, another way to get the commitment necessary is through a leader with a strong vision for change, and we'll discuss that further in a later chapter too. If there isn't a burning platform already, a senior leader often decides to light one when he or she sees a department with only 2.5 hours of explained work time per person-day!

Step 2. Measure and Analyze the Process

When we discussed the GPS story in Chapter 6, we structured that story using the Lean Six Sigma process improvement framework called DMAIC, and we explained in detail how that "structured commonsense" approach can be used to:

+ *Define* the opportunity, process, and customer requirements.
+ *Measure* the efficiency and effectiveness of the process.
+ *Analyze* the causes and impacts of opportunities within the process.
+ *Improve* the process.
+ *Control* the process to sustain the gain.

While the approach and the tools used within it have been well described in other books (including Roland's previous work in *The Six Sigma Way*), we decided to illustrate and highlight the value of the Lean Six Sigma methods as we told the GPS story because we still strongly believe that it works in many situations.

Of course, we've also illustrated Engaged Team Performance concepts that are *not* part of the Lean Six Sigma methodology, and so we hope that readers recognize that we support the value of process and data analysis but also believe that team engagement is important as well.

We discussed process analysis tools earlier, and we highly recommend the Lean tool called the Value Stream Map as a foundation for that purpose. Key components of a VSM are:

+ Value of each process step
+ Staffing for each process step
+ Volume flow rate of customer demand for products or services
+ Work time to do each step
+ Work in process (inventory) waiting before each step
+ Wait time in each inventory queue
+ Information flow to control work

The refinery had process maps, unit diagrams, piping details, and even exploded views of pumps at the ready. Creating from these a Value Stream Map of the right "altitude" was the challenge—too high, and it was "oil in here, gasoline out there"; too low, and we were mired in detail such as "this pump connected to that pipe connected to . . ."—so we resorted to the time-tested yellow stickies on the wall and mapped the core and supporting processes of the plant. These maps gave us a reference document to drive information and data gathering, and they gave everyone the opportunity to see how they fit in and how the pieces fit together. Everything that appeared relevant was attached: unit production goals and actual volumes; shift FTE counts; job descriptions; lists of tasks and responsibilities; tools needed. You name it; if it was discussed or offered, it went either on the wall or on the piles of "artifacts" on the floor under the VSM.

Although sometimes customer requirements may seem to be well known, a thorough Voice of the Customer collection effort can uncover unknown needs and priorities. A common challenge with VOC is that there will be numerous internal "experts" suggesting that the customer issues and perceptions are well known and so reaching out would be a waste of time and effort. Unfortunately, many biases are introduced this way: the "loud voice" bias (a single vocal customer issue that everyone remembers), the commingling of personal motivations with the customer's actual statement, or the potential to miss or misunderstand the needs of certain customer segments, for example.

There also might be a need to do different types of root cause and statistical analysis to unearth the key drivers of a specific problem, and many of those analytical tools are described in the Six Sigma methodology. Because other references on Lean and Six Sigma describe those methods more than adequately, we'll defer any further detail here.

After gaining an understanding of the work, the process, and the customer, the team needs to measure the outcomes of the process and the standards for work, including the time that a particular task is expected to take, called "standard time." Chapter 7 described the approach to identifying measures and gathering data. Again, other resources such as the *Six Sigma Way Team Fieldbook* offer plenty of guidance in designing measurement systems, and we'd certainly encourage readers to use those kinds of references if needed.

Step 3. Streamline the Work

We've already covered some of the basic design principles for streamlined process flow within the GPS story and other examples, but we should summarize those again here.

The first principle is *value*: the process should invest effort only in work that produces something of value for the customer.

Such work is called "value-added," and each activity should meet all three of these criteria:

1. The activity physically changes the product or service toward completion.
2. The customers would pay for the result of the activity if they knew about it.
3. The activity is done right the first time.

Obviously, activities that just prepare, move, hand off, sort, wait, transfer, check, or fix the product or service are non-value-added and can be considered waste. The Seven Wastes are often described as:

+ *Overproduction.* The product (e.g., quantity) exceeds customer requirements.

+ *Waiting.* Delays cause extra work (e.g., to update status for customers).

+ *Defects.* The product or service doesn't meet customer specifications (includes 100 percent inspection and rework of defective work products to fix it).

+ *Overprocessing.* People do more work than necessary to achieve the result (e.g., a handoff causes double work when multiple people touch the same product).

+ *Inventory/work in process.* Carrying an excess level of material, goods, or information ties up capital, creates obsolescence, or requires extra customer coordination.

+ *Transportation.* Material, information, or people are moved *between* work locations (except final delivery, if that is value-added to the customer).

+ *Motion.* There are excessive movements *within* the work location.

Before trying to right-size the process, you have to get rid of the non-value-added work, at least as much of it as you can. At that point, you're then ready to identify the right value-added process steps, put them in the right order, and pilot the new process, capturing all the details of the new process in a "to be" Value Stream Map.

The concept of mistake proofing ties into both the Lean and Six Sigma approaches that we discussed in previous chapters. Defects should be prevented if possible, detected immediately when not prevented, and measured from both a customer and internal perspective.

The next principle is *flow,* which means that the process should have just enough capacity to meet demand. As you saw from the GPS story, this principle has to be carefully applied, since most processes encounter variation in both the customer demand (e.g., a busy season or a busy day of the week) and process capacity (e.g., from equipment reliability, system outages, or absenteeism). The GPS story in Chapter 3 highlighted some of the statistical analysis tools for analyzing variation, and we'll suffice it to say that the right size for a team becomes obvious after using the right measurements and analysis techniques. In almost every situation, the team will need to establish new measurements to monitor and control sources of capacity variation, and the team members will often also need to do some brainstorming on ways to react to and influence demand variation, including ideas like variable schedules and pricing. As an example, when a restaurant issues a coupon for free kids meals that is only good on Monday, Tuesday, and Wednesday nights, it's attempting to influence demand to achieve more stable daily business volumes. Figure out how to apply that concept to your business!

Another variation on flow is called "single-piece flow"—this is really an attempt to remove handoffs by having one person complete a single piece of work before moving to another one. People have a habit of "batching" work, doing one subtask on a number of pieces of work before doing the next subtask on the batch. If you think about it, that's really a handoff to yourself! The objective in streamlining processes would be to have each piece of work touched only once, which some people call "Once & Done."

You can take that handoff reduction concept too far, however! There's a reason that lawyers hire administrative assistants: the lawyer's time is worth a lot, and handing off some tasks makes lots of sense. Sometimes a handoff is a great idea. The way to decide is fairly simple: does the benefit of the handoff (usually in cost differential of the resources doing the steps) outweigh the additional work time, double handling, extra reading, etc., that it causes? Sometimes the handoff is necessary because two different people have specialized skills that are hard to cross-train. You just have to look hard at the actual work and perhaps even pilot some cross-training to try out the concept.

Having just said that, more often we find phony reasons for handoffs, with more of the rationale being organizational history and job protection rather than a dispassionate business decision based on actual costs.

Ultimately, the best job protection comes from being flexible. Those team members who can learn new skills, take initiative to collaborate, and demonstrate autonomy when appropriate will succeed in the job market of the future. While the best teams are perhaps not perfectly cross-trained (where anyone can do anything, anywhere, any time!), strong teams like those in GPS have intentionally developed the agility to allow them to react as needed to variation in customer demand.

All this theory ties back to flow! Agility and flexibility in the workforce are key drivers of a team's capacity to deliver flow of products or services when the customer wants them.

The last concept of streamlined work is *pull*, and it's often most applicable to manufacturing operations. Pull means that the process should only create the product or service to meet a specific customer request, and many manufacturing operations have begun to apply make-to-order and just-in-time processes that use this concept to minimize the cost of carrying inventory.

Transactional processes, by definition, are usually initiated by the customer and so are almost always designed as pull systems already. It's hard to start producing a mortgage before you receive the application! If you do find that a transactional process is doing a substantial portion of the work before it has received all the information (usually from the customer) that is needed to complete the process, you'll probably also find handoffs, waiting, and rework associated with trying to do the work before the team knows everything.

Remember the rules of refining:

1. If the stuff is in the pipes or tanks, you're probably OK.

2. If it is on the ground or in the air, something is very wrong.

3. What goes in must come out (if not, refer to #2).

The refinery had been thoughtfully designed and carefully maintained and modified throughout the years, so there was no expectation that the core refining process would change. The team's charter was to analyze the numerous transactional processes that operated, maintained, staffed, and replenished the pipes, pumps, and tanks and that tested and shipped the product. The Seven Wastes and the design principles were discussed and applied, issues and opportunities surfaced, and streamlined processes emerged. This is where the atmosphere got tense. Jobs that people had been doing for years (and their fathers before them!) no longer seemed relevant. Boundaries between functional groups, particularly between operations and maintenance, were threatened—what was always "my job" looked like it would be more efficiently done by "them." The glaring searchlight of the Seven Wastes and the corresponding design principles reduced some arguments to "but . . . , but . . . , but . . . we've always done it that way!" We didn't push it; there was no point in antagonizing anyone at this point when experience shows that logic will prevail.

Slowly, the right ideas came out.

For example, the team recommended that a pipe, placed temporarily a few years ago to accommodate some maintenance and recently disconnected and slated for demolition, be reconnected and formalized, as it allowed better management of production across two units. Once the team acquired a more global view, it made perfect sense.

Step 4. Make the Work and Data Visible

Visible work is the strongest form of visual data. Roland muses on his days in manufacturing plants, "It's hard to ignore that pile of parts waiting on the workbench. The machinist knows what needs to be finished; anyone passing by can see the progress." One of the key attributes of kanban replenishment systems is that the bins containing parts are tangible, in your face—not a number buried in a report – "only five left!" is obvious to all. As we described in detail in Chapter 9, the current status of the team's work and the appropriate performance measurements need to be immediately observable by anyone and everyone in the work area in real time. Real time means that every time an item arrives to be worked, it is visible to all the team members; and as each item is completed, that event is immediately visible. Often changing the physical configuration of the team's workspace is necessary to gain visibility. For some teams that's easy, and for others it requires substantial creativity to design the layout to drive the right collaborative effects.

Information technology can often enable better work visualization; for example, many call centers have monitors that show key metrics to the entire team, but the challenge is displaying all the balanced, actionable metrics, not just the "easy" ones. Sometimes IT solutions actually make the work invisible, for instance, by deploying a workflow or imaging system that gets rid of stacks of paper and creates "work buckets" hidden in the computer system. We're not saying that those systems are bad; we're saying that those work buckets still need to be measured and displayed in real time for the team to see somewhere on a wall monitor. A daily report that's e-mailed to the team is *not* a visual control!

Our Louisiana refinery already had many electronic displays, some integrated into the control room panels, many available to workstations throughout the plant. It was relatively easy to get a summary plant production graph, with unit throughput and storage data, posted and available real time to all. The huge challenge was changing the mindset and motivators of the managers, supervisors, engineers, team leads, operators, and maintenance personnel. The team needed to look at the data from a "whole-team" perspective and care about the "whole team's" result!

The refinery physically wasn't going to be rebuilt to facilitate changes in the work, but visualizing the work caused the operators and maintenance personnel to rethink their work notification system. Previously, work requests were input by operators and queued to unit supervisors to prioritize and assign, often delaying repairs unnecessarily. The team settled on a simple operations-maintenance protocol for communicating real time the vital repairs and for queuing the less critical to a work list. This process was simple, yet effective, at keeping the whole plant producing.

Finally, we have one suggestion for helping the team see the possibilities in making the work visible and the data visual: create a pretend work area with an empty floor, and brainstorm potential layouts starting with a clean slate. Teams often unconsciously hinder themselves by feeling trapped within their existing work area, and designing a new physical configuration in an empty conference room, basement, or warehouse can allow them to think in new ways about the layout.

Step 5. Organize the Team

After understanding, measuring, streamlining, and visualizing the work, the team can create a staffing model using the multiple regression equation or Functional Review approach. Working from the "to be" Value Stream Map from Step 3, identify skill sets necessary to perform the tasks (trying to ignore the process step blocks, which are artificial and probably obsolete boundaries), and see if there are clumps of tasks that readily become a "job." Consider the possibility of additional training, bringing new skills into new, more holistic jobs. Old paradigms will be hard to break ("a CSR has always done that!"), but the benefits are tremendous. We've seen occasions where mundane tasks have been added to a more expensive resource's job because the cost and time delay associated with the handoff and restart were greater. The staffing model will need to take into account these new job descriptions, and so the regression model may have to be adapted or estimates made.

As the members of the refinery team began to coalesce, they began to acknowledge that the boundaries between operator's duties and those of maintenance were artificial and hindering their working together as a team (you can't do that task, because the wrench required is over 8 inches!) and that the whole "supervisor as gatekeeper" concept was an obstacle.

After days of drawing many process maps with yellow stickies on the walls, we were beginning the second day of a skills-jobs-structure design session. We'd ended the previous day deliberately open-ended—there had been much discussion about skills, job boundaries, and supervisory and management structure, building on the team's recent "discovery" of the negative impact of the existing unit structure. The usual greetings, coffee, and milling about, and we were under way, beginning to construct elements of jobs and structure around the core process. Progress was slow; no one wanted to offend, to rock the boat, to suggest that a friend's or relative's job might have been unnecessary all these years.

An older gentleman, seemingly respected and deferred to by many in this working group, was unusually quiet, withdrawn.

"What's up, Harry?" we inquired.

"Oh, nuttin'," he drawled in finest Cajun.

"Com'on, Harry; you're not your usual self—you OK?" we pressed.

"Well, I couldn't sleep last night, bothered by all these maps and ideas. I got up hours ago ..."—looooong pregnant pause—and then he continued, "I sketched out an idea I had; nuttin' much."

"Where is it? Can we see it?" we asked.

"Well, I don't really want to show it; might get in trouble for some of the conclusions I came to. It's in my truck."

We took a short break while he brought it in—a piece of poster paper (probably fish wrap) with boxes and lines and arrows neatly describing (we thought) a nearly perfect high-performance work teams design. "Wow," we thought. "They're gonna kill him."

He sheepishly began to explain his "nightmare" to the assembled company, who listened attentively. After responding to some clarifying questions, much to his surprise (and our delight!), one of the participants who had been typically more skeptical and critical of our process and the discussions so far said, "Perfect! I think we're all done now," and received a chorus of "ayes." We adjusted our agenda and spent the rest of the day testing and validating the assumptions in his design, delivering a final result not far from what he had posted at 8:30 that morning.

After the breakthrough to come up with a new organization design, it's almost always necessary to pilot the new process with a single team to confirm the new capacity after all the process changes have been identified. In doing that pilot, the team will often discover new ways of working together, collaborative norms that they will need to apply to match up with the new processes, measures, and visual controls.

Fluid Form organization, which we mentioned numerous times and described in more detail in a previous chapter, is a visionary concept, more of a journey than a destination. The team should begin to identify ways to evolve its formal reporting structure to match the new realities of decentralized decision making, individual accountability for supporting team goals, and team-focused drive for results. As the GPS team leader observed after the team had finished its ETP transformation, when the team learns to manage itself to meet the customers' needs, the team leader needs to supervise less and can become more proactive about improving the process and developing the team members.

Step 6. Set Team Goals

Hopefully we've also covered the rationale for setting team goals in sufficient depth. Together, goals and work distribution methods that directly relate to meeting a customer-required outcome *as a team* form the key driver of the collaboration that leads to Engaged Team Performance.

Customers of the refinery want the right product in the right amount in the right pipe at the right time. Shipments are scheduled, pipeline capacity is reserved, tankage is managed, and unit or plant upsets or delays are extremely disruptive. A unit "getting ahead" is just as bad as one "getting behind" because the extra product has nowhere to go!

With consistent flow as the plant team goal, a shared understanding of the contribution and impact of each unit, and a real-time visual display of performance in comparison to the goal available to all, the unit teams could now coordinate to deliver continuously. On a more individual level, accountability took two forms. First, the members of the team had to perform to deliver the team goals, which required refinements to the performance management system. No longer was the supervisor the sole judge of an individual's performance; the team had input. Second, the individuals could choose to take on more responsibility, to learn more tasks, increasing their breadth of capability, hence their versatility. It was a long and bumpy transition.

By the way, when we argue for removing most individual *goals*, we're not advocating the removal of individual *accountabilities*. Ultimately, each person should be evaluated on his or her contributions to the team. Those individuals who deliver more value should be retained, developed, promoted, and rewarded appropriately. And unfortunately, those individuals who can't meet a minimum standard of performance should find other roles, either within or outside the organization. Leaders must recognize that while all people deserve equal treatment and opportunity, all people are *not* created with equal abilities; there will always be some variation in performance, and the leadership team should be able to define the minimum acceptable result (separately from the expected typical, average, standard performance) without making that minimum an individual goal for everyone!

While the nuances in the statements above are complex, readers should now be able to differentiate between a standard and a goal. That's an accountability for readers who want to read on, so if you didn't get it, go back and read it again!

Step 7. Lead the Transition

We've discussed a number of times the concept of piloting the new process in order to enhance the process concept, establish norms, and measure the new capacity of the team before expanding the changes to everyone. While we almost always do a pilot for these reasons, we often encounter a critical challenge: the pilot team may believe that failure is an easy way to go back to the status quo. When the whole organization buys into the burning platform in Step 1, that's not a problem. Unlike old John Wayne navy movies, however, there isn't often a way to burn the lifeboats during a process transformation effort, and sometimes the proposed changes seem scary; so the leadership team has to communicate that the purpose of the pilot is to decide "*how* to make the new process work, not *if* we're going to do it."

We guided the refinery team through a change of mindset from analyzing, debating, and designing to planning the transition and implementation. The plant manager congratulated the team members on their new design, and reminded them that this was necessary for survival, that it wasn't optional, and that he understood that it couldn't be changed overnight. He charged them to view it as a "turnaround"—the name the industry uses for the upgrade or overhaul of some or all of the plant. Turnarounds typically span many (sometimes many, many) months and are meticulously planned and analyzed for risks before a valve is turned or a pipe severed. Their plan included many "offline" changes, that is, process and organization changes that affected support processes but did not touch the flow of oil. These were assessed for "reversibility"—could they be unwound if performance was not what was expected? If so, implementation was straightforward and rapid. "Online" changes were phased. A unit volunteered to pilot the operations-maintenance team design, one shift, then all, carefully measured and tuned. The adjoining units came next, rolling out in a wave through the whole plant.

Another critical piece of advice: you have to *underresource the pilot* in order to find out how fast it really can go. When a team is overresourced, the people sometimes find other "important" work to do rather than going beyond what they perceive as the daily goal, and their past knowledge of the previous process may subconsciously discourage the team from pressing to get more done. We called that the "room in your garage effect" in a previous discussion. Fortunately, the pilot team members usually have some prior connection to the project team anyway, and so they're often willing to try the new process wholeheartedly.

Then it's time to expand the process to the entire department, and that's when the real fun begins . . . The transition frequently requires substantial role definition, cross-training, reorganization, and perhaps even staffing-level changes, all of which can be challenging for leaders and their teams. It's a heck of a lot of work.

Often the improvements in Engaged Team Performance continue to evolve gradually as teams become fully trained and the team goals and norms begin to drive different behaviors. So, while it's possible that the initial reorganization will result in staffing-level changes, most companies find other roles for the small numbers of initially displaced people, and much of the real staffing reductions are accomplished through attrition over time rather than through layoffs. Sometimes when a company is growing, the existing staff stays the same and just gets more work done, which usually translates to getting higher revenues from customers. That said, we never promise at the beginning of an ETP effort that there *won't* be a layoff; everyone has to be candid and aware that the company's leaders will make the best business decision possible and then execute it in the most compassionate way that they can.

No one lost his or her job at the refinery, but as retirements and attrition occurred, not all positions were retained. Often one of the most difficult systems to alter is how performance is managed—typically the human resources department owns the process and either controls or strongly influences the rules. In this case, a key member of the refinery's centralized HR organization was a project sponsor and strong advocate of the new design, which enabled the transition.

Step 8. Sustain the Team's Performance

While all the previously discussed streamlined processes, visual measures, team goals, collaborative norms, and organizational designs are critical to *sustain*, we have found that the word *sustain* can lull a team into a false sense of security. The reality is that if you're not getting better, you're probably getting worse! So we encourage teams to sustain their Engaged Team Performance by continually trying to improve it.

Our refinery viewed its project as the beginning of an adventure—continually looking for opportunities to streamline, flatten, motivate, and improve the efficiency and effectiveness of safely delivering lowest-cost refined oil. The risks of relapse are many: new management, new or transferring (and potentially more influential) employees, a significant rise in the price of oil (there goes the burning platform!), a new owner, or even a change in the crude source (different oil = different process = different organization, to some).

As we remarked in an earlier chapter, Sociotechnical Systems have a high rate of recidivism without appropriate leadership and good controls. A simple, public, fast, and reliable system for measuring and displaying the fundamentals is critical. Although it's easy to argue about "what changed" after the fact, it is hard to argue with data—a downward trend in production and an upward trend in cost should immediately trigger analysis, although in a true ETP environment the production teams will likely have already figured it out and gotten things back on track!

We've shown a number of time-ordered trend charts in some of our examples, and we'd like to briefly reinforce that ongoing measurements need to be designed that way. We highly recommend a book on that topic by Donald Wheeler called *Understanding Variation*. It's not as statistical as it sounds, and it's a concise discussion of the most important thing that people need to know about data: *observing data as a trend chart over time allows leaders and teams to differentiate between a real process issue, a significant one-time event, and the typical "noise" of random variation.*

Most companies are managed from PFN (pages full of numbers), which can enable two behaviors: (1) reacting unnecessarily to the usual random variation and (2) not acting on an important trend or event. Quite often we see what we refer to as "three-point data"—this month, last month, and this month last year. The three charts in Figure 13-2 all have the same data points for January and February this year and February last year; however, we're willing to guess that you interpret them as highly different (recovery, random variation, and a slow slide downhill). Three points don't tell any of the three stories well!

An interesting paradox to consider is that when most people invest their own hard-earned money in the stock market, they will study the charts on their favorite trading sites; however, they are satisfied to manage at work using PFN. It may take a little more effort to convert the data to graphs, but they can be a real eye-opener.

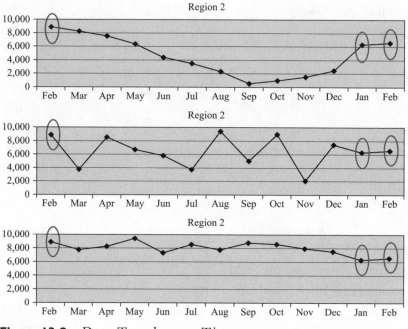

Figure 13-2   Data Trends over Time

And then leaders and team members need to watch the data, listen to the customer, analyze the process, develop the people, and continue to sustain high performance and drive future improvements.

Once a team has transitioned to Engaged Team Performance, the greatest threat is that a new manager (or even worse, a new consultant!) will try to change things back. While managing an efficient, effective, engaged team sounds like fun, it can really get boring when there are no problems for the leader to swoop in and solve. The leaders need to have the maturity to understand their own roles and let the team members do theirs.

One last caution: once a team has achieved the efficiency from being a right-staffed engaged team, it doesn't have the ability to continue to "cut 10 percent" every year without changing the process! If some of the senior leaders up the chain are still playing the sandbagging game and try to cut the staffing of an efficient team, they'll cause a performance crash. And that's a great segue to the next chapter, where we'll discuss the senior leader's role in ETP.

Chapter Summary

The basic steps to achieve Engaged Team Performance are:

1. *Commit to change.* Find a burning platform for change.
2. *Measure and analyze the process.* Investigate the current process and customer requirements, and measure outcomes and work standards.
3. *Streamline the work.* Improve the flow of the process to deliver value efficiently.
4. *Make the work and data visible.* Make the new work processes, collaborative norms, and control measures visually obvious in the workplace.
5. *Organize the team.* Reorganize and right-size the team for the work.
6. *Set team goals.* Assess team performance and establish team goals.
7. *Lead the transition.* Make a rational plan and develop the skills, tools, systems, and knowledge to move the team to the envisioned future state.
8. *Sustain Engaged Team Performance.* Demonstrate performance over time!

The Path Forward

The Role of Senior Leadership in Enabling Engaged Team Performance

So FAR, WE have devoted most of our writing to providing help to team and departmental-level leaders who get the work done in organizations everywhere, but now we'd like to close by highlighting the critical role that senior leadership has in *enabling* Engaged Team Performance.

Vision and Benchmarking

Stephen Covey quite rightly says that you should always "begin with the end in mind," and so while we know that the concept of vision has been described in extensive detail in other books as well, we'd like to offer some short reminders about it here.

Senior leaders are critical shapers and sharers of a vision for the future. In the previous chapter, we discussed the importance of finding a burning platform to drive the high level of commitment for doing all the work that will be necessary to transition to ETP. The best leaders are able to quickly get past the dry description of the financial and business value of their intended future state—leaders have to describe victory in personal and emotional terms. People need to know how ETP *feels*.

Engaged Team Performance produces winners. At the end of a football game, two exhausted teams leave the field. Both have worked hard, and both have left blood and sweat on the field (hopefully no tears). But there's a big difference between one exit tunnel and the other: one team is happy, and the other is dejected.

Have you ever been on the dejected team at work? That's the team where everyone works hard and can't understand why the customers aren't satisfied. Perhaps the relationship with customers has even spiraled down to distrust and dislike. On that team, everyone looks over his or her shoulder to make sure other folks are working just as hard. Work is distributed individually to make sure it's "fair" to everyone. Relationships among team members are strained, and the employee-management relationship is even worse. The team's area looks messy and hectic, with almost a frenzy of activity, yet without the hope of the right result.

On the dejected team, leaders think they have to police the people. They monitor breaks, make hourly trips to see who's in the smoking area, watch Internet usage, and take away paperback novels from people who should be working. We know; we remember being those leaders, and it wasn't fun.

In contrast, the Engaged Team hums quietly. There is activity, but never panic. The work flows visibly. The people collaborate. Customer interactions are overwhelmingly positive. The team maintains work-life balance. The team members get all the work done, and the team members police themselves instead of making management watch them. Others visit them to see what their secret is.

Like visioning, benchmarking is a great concept that can sometimes get overdone, but one excellent way to envision the future of ETP is to visit someone else who's already doing it. We know of four highly successful Engaged Team Performance change efforts in the last three years that have started with a tour of the GPS work area. One of those new areas is now giving tours to other teams as well.

Proactive Management of Expectations

One of the major stressors associated with changes in the workplace is fear of job loss (change = layoffs, right?). Although the younger generations will likely react with less passion, many still have families, car payments, and mortgages to worry about. Managing the uncertainty surrounding possible "reductions in force" that might occur as a result of a streamlining activity can reduce or alleviate this stress.

Recent economic forces have not encouraged much contemplation of action, rather an atmosphere of reaction: the corporate leaders on high get together behind closed doors and determine how many heads need to roll, and then they cascade the orders; then departments make the cuts and struggle to clean up the mess. This usually results in broken processes, dissatisfied customers, and overworked, disgruntled survivors.

If time and economics allow, we're advocating essentially three phases: sort out the process so it delivers what the customers want efficiently; align the team and the goals to drive the right behaviors; and finally, make the changes in staff. The customers will feel an immediate improvement in their experience, while the employees will be engaged in designing and transitioning to their future state. If there is a need to reduce head count, attrition may take some, a few may decide that this new environment isn't their piece of cake, and the real "right size" and right skills mix will be obvious. Reducing the stress by lessening the threat associated with an announcement can smooth the kickoff and transition.

We're not suggesting making any commitment, rather providing an explanation of the possibilities. People want honesty, however painful, and the younger folks, particularly Gen Y, want context. "We need to do this because..." "We want you to participate in..." "It is possible that..." "It is expected that you will design a simpler process supported by the right skills..." "No guarantees of..." Key individuals can be counseled privately about their specific roles, in both the project and the future environment. All the relevant possibilities should be discussed—skills growth, attrition, transfer, and separation.

The surprising thing we've experienced is that most people are willing to participate fairly, even with enthusiasm, in the project even though they know that they may not be part of the final process team. Once in a while a few team members will "paint a bulls-eye on their own chests" (nominate themselves for corrective action or dismissal) by misbehaving, and swift, decisive action will earn the respect of the rest. Some will try to protect their turf through misrepresentation of the facts and will be discovered from the data analysis or refuted by the rest of the team.

The bottom line: if there is sufficient time, have an open discussion about the possible outcomes of the project, and expect the respect shown by that effort to be rewarded with reduced stress and better engagement in the effort.

Functional Review

Most companies have some type of "operational review" process for senior leaders to get strategic performance reports from their departments. Processes for managing performance vary greatly from company to company, of course, but here are a few testimonials:

+ *Plan on a Page.* Scott Bajtos at VMware has used a "Plan on a Page" concept to encourage teams to focus their measures, goals, and action plans down to a concise plan. Teams are limited to eight key performance indicators (measures) and five key initiatives. Scott says that the plans help the company to "sustain great results in an ever-changing, fast-paced environment." The Plan on a Page has four components, very similar to Kaplan and Norton's Balanced Scorecard, with customer, employee, operational excellence, and financial categories.

  At a previous company, Cameron Karr developed a comprehensive customer surveying process for Scott's team that, combined with the one-page plan, drove over 60 percent increases in customer satisfaction for some teams, while reducing labor in customer support by 22 percent. In support of the Plan on a Page concept, Scott's managers were compensated for improving customer satisfaction. At first, they had improvement goals but didn't have the tools they needed to drive change. Scores went up dramatically when they gave managers access to real-time feedback at the engineer level so they knew who was performing well and when to shift resources. As one manager said, "We finally have a playbook so we can hit our performance goals."

+ *The five-page plan.* Jane Stackpole at Silicon Valley Bank uses a five-page plan. Her approach to monitoring performance of the business starts with comprehensive data about the customer experience, supplemented by market research and segmented by type of customer relationship. Working with Adaptive Path, each type of customer was

given a "persona"—making each "customer" come to life
with a name and key personal traits. Her team uses regression analysis to understand the drivers behind the customers' performance ratings of the company. She says that
SVB's client experience program is an ongoing effort, not
a project: "It's a journey, not a destination."

Everyone has a different name for this kind of presentation,
but what we'll call the Functional Review approach provides a
way that leaders can identify the potential gains from ETP, begin
to find a burning platform for change, and monitor their departments' progress in implementing the concepts. The Functional
Review is an opportunity to quickly study each business process
in the company, collect effectiveness and efficiency data, identify opportunities to improve, and present the entire package as
a 90-minute briefing from the department's director to the senior
leadership team.

By setting up a *routine process for leaders to regularly assess and
report* a set of standard effectiveness and efficiency measures, the
senior team can make informed decisions about resources and
investment in change opportunities. Many of you may recognize
this concept as an evolution of a dashboard of measures, and most
companies have tried to put some kind of dashboard in place,
perhaps even following the principles from Kaplan and Norton's
acclaimed book, *The Balanced Scorecard*. Sometimes these efforts
have worked, but many times they've died out over time. The
main cause for failures we've observed was that departments
would create the measures and then nobody would *do* anything
with them.

The Functional Review is different in that it creates a regular forum for those measures to be discussed and converted into
action. Without the Functional Review's demand for department
leaders to brief the numbers occasionally to the senior leadership
team, the charts become wallpaper. We recommend a quarterly
update and briefing of the measures, with connections to other

critical leadership activities such as the strategic planning, annual budgeting, performance planning, and information technology queue management processes. Some companies do larger briefings less frequently, and some brief a one-page plan monthly; regardless, the demand to brief performance measures can drive critical engagement in department-level leadership.

In early 2007, the leaders of a division of the Principal Financial Group® took the GPS team's example and made it into a template for replicating the Functional Review across their business. In the prior year, they had executed Functional Reviews informally, without using a standard reporting template, by simply having meetings with the finance team and each department's director to identify opportunities and review budget commitments for the next year. But the project storyboard presentation from the GPS improvement project gave them a solid start to a template, and so they deployed a 30-page PowerPoint presentation document across the division with a mandate from senior leadership for each director to deliver an initial review by midyear.

All departments were given an example template with the actual GPS data, a blank template for their own Functional Review presentation, and a day with the consulting team to create their data collection plan. While the distributed templates were standardized, the leadership team emphasized that each department would need to figure out how to apply the measurements and concepts to its particular processes, and obviously some areas would have a different focus than others.

The senior leadership team told all departments that they would have to play, and they put actual dates on the calendar for two to three months out, when the department leaders would be expected to deliver their Functional Review presentations to the executive team. While it had been hard to get leaders to schedule the informal reviews in the prior year, the simple act of putting a briefing to the senior vice president on their calendars gave the department leaders all the momentum they

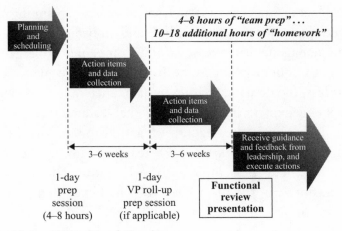

Figure 14-1 Functional Review

needed this time. Amazing, isn't it? The diagram in Figure 14-1 shows the major preparation activities and timeline.

The basic components of the Functional Review presentation template are:

+ High-level processes and department's fit within the organization

+ Customers' critical requirements

+ Measures of effectiveness in delivering to customer requirements

+ Measures of efficiency in use of internal resources

+ Staffing and organization (including org chart and staffing model)

+ Opportunities to adjust staffing to react to changes in capacity and demand

+ Performance management methods and scores of teams and individuals

+ Department budget and financial results

+ Current efforts to improve performance and results (with status updates)

+ Potential new opportunities to launch improvement projects

We won't include detailed descriptions of all the above measures, and we adequately described the core concepts of measuring effectiveness and efficiency in Chapter 7, but we'd like to illustrate one of the key tools that the team found useful, which we call the "efficiency snapshot."

Figure 14-2 is the actual efficiency snapshot of the GPS team, taken in March 2007, six months after the initial process improvement efforts were completed, but in the midst of the improvements that the team eventually achieved in performance. Note that the "total staff on hand" (on the second line from the bottom) was 48 at this time, though the staff eventually got down to 38 people a year later.

The snapshot is simply an automated "napkin" to help a team or department calculate its own magic equation! It's a spreadsheet-based tool that allows a team to plug in its work volumes and timing (top half) and staffing (bottom half) to drive calculations of efficiency.

				Most recent month:	
Efficiency snapshot				*March, 2007*	
Outputs should match high-level process reported:	Output 1:	Output 2:	Output 3: (etc.)	Department Total:	Workforce Efficiency:
Unit of volume	Quotes				
Volume per month	6,280				
Work time in minutes (weighted average): *actual time study*	25.20				
Standard work time per month (minutes)	158,256			158,256	
Workdays in most recent month	21.00				
Standard work time per day (hours)	125.6			125.60	
Nonproductive time (productivity gap!)				103.20	
Direct labor hours = remaining paid hours per day				228.80	54.90%
Remaining labor for direct production				28.6	59.58%
Training: include trainers and trainee FTE not in production				5.0	10.42%
Indirect support (quality review, expert coaches, etc.)				4.0	8.33%
Project support (list projects; nonleader)				2.6	5.42%
PTO and VTO taken in most recent month (nonleader)				2.3	4.79%
NonPTO paid leave FTE (nonleader FMLA, etc.)				1.5	3.13%
Leadership and management staff				4.0	8.33%
Total staff on hand (FTE) from org chart				48.0	100.0%
Total available hours per day in most recent month				384	32.71%

Figure 14-2   Efficiency Snapshot

On the top part of the chart, the department must list its major process outputs or deliverables, and then measure both the quantity and the average work time to produce each type of output. In the example in the figure, we used monthly volumes, and the calculations within the spreadsheet are designed to get to a number of labor hours "earned" per day. You'll recognize that "standard work time" per day is a key concept from earlier in the book. Some departments have one or just a few outputs like the GPS quotes in the figure, but many departments have many more; we've created snapshots for departments with more complex tasks that had 20 to 25 columns in the top section, which add up all the deliverables to summarize the total explained work.

The bottom half of the chart allows the department to differentiate between the time invested in "direct labor" (people doing production work) and indirect labor (support teams, personal time off, etc.) by separating the amount of effort spent on nonproduction activities.

The chart ultimately produces two measurements:

+ *Overall workforce efficiency (OWE)*. The amount of work-time credit divided by the total staffing, which includes support and leadership overhead

+ *Direct labor efficiency (DLE)*. The amount of work-time credit divided by the total staffing "available and assigned to production"

You can see that in early 2007 the GPS team had overall workforce efficiency of 32.7 percent and direct labor efficiency of 54.9 percent. In contrast, data from other sources show that departmental teams typically have OWE of 15 to 20 percent and DLE of 30 to 40 percent. The GPS department today operates with OWE of about 50 percent and DLE of about 75 percent. Try this with your own department—if you can explain 60 to 70 percent of your production staffing and 40 to 50 percent of your total staffing based on completion credit from standard work-time and actual volumes, you're doing well.

Most departments can't. That's why senior leaders need Functional Reviews. When it comes time to make important strategic decisions, perhaps even the budget cuts and layoffs that we've seen in the last recession, leaders often lack the critical information that they need. And so they're left to make the decision in the only "fair" way that they can: they ask each subordinate department to give up 10 percent (or whatever number) across the board. That approach unfortunately "rewards the guilty and punishes the innocent" while perpetuating bad behaviors like sandbagging.

An Organizational Approach to ETP

Perhaps obviously, the Functional Review approach we've described can become a great lead-in to Step 1, building a case for the organization to *commit to change*. Senior leaders and their teams can see the processes, performance, and relative opportunities of multiple departments side by side, and then they can prioritize efforts to improve their results. The Functional Review can also help showcase the gains from initial ETP efforts by allowing senior leaders to compare efficient, effective teams to other groups that haven't yet made the leap.

Or senior executives can just pick up a book and decide "I want to do ETP here!" and start from the beginning with an organizational change effort.

Consequently, while Engaged Team Performance is ultimately deployed at the departmental level, senior leaders often see its impact and decide to implement the approach across larger organizations. Sometimes a senior leader will just commit to driving ETP across an organization, and other times a good "pilot" of the ETP approach, like the initial effort at GPS, can convince leaders to expand the effort. Either way, a senior leader has to decide to give it a push.

And then the leader waves a magic wand, and ETP propagates through the organization like a shock wave, instantly creating breakthrough results!

Not exactly.

It takes a concerted push, led by change agents who know how to facilitate process and performance improvement efforts, who understand ETP, and who employ strong project management skills. Luckily, most organizations actually have some of these people available, either designing systems in their information technology groups or perhaps spearheading process improvement efforts in a Lean Six Sigma support team. Sometimes a mid-level leader or two with previous experience can be freed up temporarily to help drive the change. Regardless, someone has to lead the effort, and it's hard for the department head to do that as an additional responsibility. As we discussed in Chapter 7, it's best to find a neutral facilitator to lead the project.

Some organizations also choose to hire external consulting support, usually with the intention of getting some initial results and transfer skills to internal resources along the way. The balance between "getting results" and "transferring skills" should certainly be tailored to the situation and priorities of each organization. That balance is important; too much training may miss opportunities to drive results more quickly, while too much consulting will leave the organization without continuity when the consultants leave.

A comparison of two potential approaches is shown in Figure 14-3. A consultative approach in a single department takes almost as much effort but gets results faster, while a "training and coaching" approach leverages the invested effort across more teams but proceeds a little more slowly. Both are viable alternatives, depending on the number of departments involved, the internal resources available, and the timing of the intended results.

The timing often turns out to be an important issue. Many companies use an initial ETP effort to "self-fund" change, allowing the first deployment in one department to free up capacity and then reinvesting that capacity and/or money into future efforts. Most companies try to at least break even in the first year, and that

	Single team	*Multiple teams*
Build a vision	Executive and champion project scoping (2–4 hours)	Executive overview (1 day); Champions workshop (2 days)
Scope the effort	Rapid assessment for single project deployment (1 day)	Rapid assessment for strategic deployment (2–4 days)
Launch the deployment	Project execution (23–30 days, spread over 2–4 months)	Project definition (1–2 days); Project team workshops (16–20 days per workshop, up to 4 teams)
Sustain and internalize the infrastructure	Department and team ETP certification (free)	Ongoing project coaching (1–2 days per project per month); department and team ETP certification (free)
Total effort	1 project, 24–32 days, 2–4 months	4 projects, 25–60 days, 3–6 months

Figure 14-3   ETP Deployment Options

sometimes affects the intended timing. For example, starting an ETP deployment in October can result in spending money and time in the current year that isn't paid back until the following year. Consequently, many companies try to front-load their investments in consulting and/or training into the first six months of the year so that the gains can pay back the investment by the end of that year. Over time, organizations should get more than a 5:1 hard financial payback on their investments in ETP, in addition to the softer but still critical benefit of having engaged employees. For that reason, many organizations are able to invest just for the long term regardless of the annual budget, but it's an unfortunate reality that others have to think shorter term and stay budget neutral.

One way or the other, in a single department or across a wider organization, an ETP deployment can achieve amazing results.

We must caution, however, that ETP isn't the only tool set that an organization may need to use in order to drive change. Companies may need process skills like "root cause analysis" to solve specific problems or strategy tools like "process diligence" to assess and integrate a potential acquisition. As we said in an earlier chapter, ETP is not a hammer, and not every opportunity is a nail!

Often that need for diverse skills will drive an organization to centralize a team that provides change management, process and performance improvement, and other "internal consulting" services. While that kind of team often starts out tailored to a company's specific needs, it often turns out to develop a similar set of diverse skills. Most important, it can become a great breeding ground for future leadership talent. We highly recommend that every company create such a team!

A Program for Change

After the success of the initial process improvement projects and Functional Reviews, the division at the Principal Financial Group® created a Center of Excellence (COE) and tasked the new team to more formally approach change initiatives. The COE recruited an internal team, initially supported by external consultants. The senior leadership put the former GPS director and the strategy director (the two leaders who chartered the original GPS project) in charge of the new team, and they began to execute a few key "end-to-end" projects that crossed organizational boundaries, using the gains from their initial projects to continue to invest in a number of training events, coaching relationships, and project implementations. In the next few years, the effort drove a substantial impact on the business.

While there are many important aspects to setting up a successful process and performance improvement program, the most critical by far is the objective: the effort must be clearly focused on getting breakthrough business results. As soon as the goal becomes "number of people trained and certified" or some other nonfinancial impact, the company will find better places to invest time and money.

Rather than choosing an off-the-shelf program (Lean Six Sigma training the "sheep-dip" way), we always recommend taking a tailored approach after reviewing the company's strategic imperatives.

Here's an example of the diversity of tool sets from the plan devised by the Center of Excellence for the insurance division:

Change	Tool/Technique
Enable leaders to build capacity and capability into their function	*Functional Review and budget guidance:* Continual tactical changes in a department
Enable division or segment to take nonstaff cost out	*Cost Action Teams (CATS) WorkOut:* 2–3 days plus 30- and 60-day follow-up
Create process improvement, primarily within one function	*Lean WorkOut process streamlining:* 4–6 days plus follow-on control actions
Improve the timing, cost, or quality of an existing value stream. Change could include offshoring or outsourcing or onshoring or insourcing of process components or automation of process tools using information systems	*Lean Six Sigma projects:* End-to-end core process optimization, including transactional Lean and other techniques closely associated with Six Sigma
Understand customers' changing needs and innovate!	*Process design or redesign:* End-to-end core process renewal or greenfield development, often involving new information systems

One of our colleagues, Deirdre Gengenbach, likes to say, "In order to teach someone to fish, I usually just take them fishing." Over the next few years, the COE took all of the above approaches to execute different improvement efforts, usually executing a project or two with external consulting support *before* training its internal team members on the applicable techniques in order to reinforce the capacity for sustaining internal execution of each type of project. While this sounds like a counterintuitive approach (do, then learn!), it helped the company get great early results that funded the ongoing efforts.

As of 2009, the division retained only a strategic coaching role for external consultants, who were busy writing a book anyway, and all other efforts had been internalized. When last seen, Deb Blackman was leading the Center of Excellence to drive an ETP effort to vastly reorganize the group insurance new business administration teams around a customer-focused service model called "Field Focused Teams" with single-piece flow processes.

Jenifer Moses, one of the field leaders, says of the new project: "Everyone, including the field and the home office teams, went into it certain that it was the other people who needed to change. This is the first time that I've seen an initiative where *everyone* had to do something different and everyone liked it. And the big winner was the customer."

We have little doubt that the effort will revolutionize the division's efficiency and effectiveness. And we are confident that the team is putting in the processes, measures, visual controls, team goals, norms, and organization to deliver Engaged Team Performance in the new group.

Process and Value Stream Management

There have been quite a number of books hitting the shelves of the business section lately about "process management and maturity" and other similar theories like "business architecture" design. The general idea of process management is right-on: organizations should measure, manage, and improve cross-functional *processes* instead of departments. The trouble with process management is that it takes a long time to develop the cross-functional measures and get them in place; and with accountability dispersed in different departments, it's hard to get people to work on the effort.

With the buzz it gets, you'd think that we'd have seen more positive experiences with process management by now.

We find that Engaged Team Performance transitions and implementation of Functional Reviews are great first steps toward process and performance maturity and even Fluid Form organization. After the experience of streamlining lower-level processes, engaging people, and reporting performance in a standard way, an organization is much more capable of taking the next step in driving that same approach through larger divisions that have multiple processes and functions involved.

Information Technology Systems, Sourcing, and Shoring

There are a few people out there who think that all process improvement involves fielding a new computer system. We've demonstrated a few times already in this book that teams can vastly improve both process and performance without necessarily doing anything new with their computer systems, but we'd certainly like to acknowledge that sometimes an opportunity to deploy new information technology becomes a game-changing event for a business. That kind of opportunity should and often does reap great rewards.

Or not.

For every successful system implementation, there are a couple of horror stories about a new computer system that caused issues for customers or reduced operational capacity of the process. Actually, a more typical failure mode for a systems implementation is called "paving the cow-path"—investing a large-scoped, time-consuming, and expensive effort to field a new computer system that simply automates an inefficient process, replicating useless manual steps inside a computer. Replacing a process that "makes junk" with a new computer system that "makes junk faster" isn't process improvement!

Unfortunately, the systems deployment isn't the worst opportunity to screw up a process. That honor belongs to the "shoring or sourcing" decision; you know, that's the brilliant idea where a process gets moved to a foreign country or hired out to another company, where it'll certainly be cheaper than doing it here ourselves, right? This kind of "strategy" project is often proposed by, you guessed it, a consultant. In fact, there are some consulting companies that specialize in in-sourcing, out-sourcing, off-shoring, near-shoring (even re-shoring when the latter didn't meet expectations), and other efforts with similar names. Sometimes that strategy is a good one and works well, but like a systems deployment gone wrong, an off-shoring effort can often just mimic an inefficient and ineffective process more cheaply while uncovering problems that will irritate customers even more. The fundamental concept for evaluating these options is the transaction cost, as given to us by Ronald Coase, which we discussed in Chapter 12.

The good news is, after you've finished experiencing the problems with off-shoring or out-sourcing, your process can become a great candidate for in-sourcing! The consultant you used for the previous project can probably help.

The answer, quite simply, is to combine process analysis, process improvement, system deployment, and sourcing decisions into a single strategy that incorporates Engaged Team Performance into whatever the final organizational design turns out to be. In order to do that effectively, however, the project team needs to analyze the process, measures, and customer needs before deploying the new system or moving the process to a different location. A simple way to visualize that approach is shown in Figure 14-4.

An off-shoring effort will often require new information technology, such as an image and workflow system to transmit the work from the place that the mail arrives to the place that the work will be done. Both off-shoring projects and information technology deployments should leverage a deep look at the

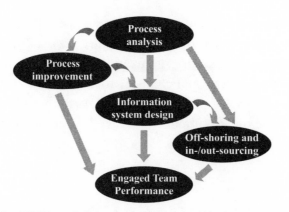

Figure 14-4   ETP and Strategic Change Options

existing process and customer requirements before designing a new solution anyway. And so if you're going to invest all the time to study the process, deploy new technology, or move processes overseas, why wouldn't you apply the rest of the ETP concepts to get the most out of your investment?

Audit and Certification

After deploying the right processes, supported by the right technology and located in the right places, one more spin on the Functional Review concept can help to standardize and sustain the organization's performance by providing external support for an audit or certification of the departments. General Electric's corporate audit staff is legendary as a breeding ground for expert evaluators of business strategy, efficiency, and effectiveness, and those audits provide a great service to the departments: they allow access to a neutral expert who can evaluate the team's progress toward the vision and coach the leadership team. The audit staff also becomes a great place to grow new leaders.

One of the benefits of deploying a standard method like ETP is the opportunity to validate leaders, team members, and process improvement project managers as "ETP Certified" practitioners. Certification helps to assure repeatable execution of the approach across an organization, and it's often included as a component of a formal change program. Obviously, certification also allows senior leaders to recognize those leaders who are driving the development of Engaged Team Performance in the organization.

Stay Out of the Way!

A number of cautions have been laced throughout this book, most of which are intended to prevent leaders from interfering with their engaged teams' performance. ETP requires teams to behave differently, and it also requires leaders to lead differently. Engaged teams are easier to motivate but harder to stretch, and they need to be resourced, measured, developed, and sustained rather than supervised. It's a sad fact that some teams can't make the jump to ETP, but it feels even worse when a leader can't make the shift to *leading* ETP.

Experience teaches leaders that they need to be heroes; many of them have risen through the ranks because they were the stars of the team. But in order to be a good coach for an engaged team, the leader needs to be comfortable sitting on the bench.

A Note for Leaders Acquiring Responsibility for an ETP Team

Many leaders who find themselves acquiring responsibility for an existing workforce feel that they have to change something, to "make their mark" on the organization. Tread lightly with an ETP team, we suggest. Imposing traditional management and supervision practices will quickly disengage the team members, resulting in loss of the performance gains. Even altering the metrics is likely to have unintended consequences, leading to unproductive behaviors and reduced efficiency and effectiveness.

Take time to study all aspects: the layout, norms, process, metrics, personalities, and social structure, as well as the results they deliver, both internally and for their customers. Reread Part I of this book to review some of the historical precedents and concepts that are the foundation of ETP. Interview the team members collectively and individually to hear about the journey that they traveled to become an engaged team, and above all, tread lightly.

Chapter Summary

+ Senior leaders need to drive Engaged Team Performance by setting a vision for the transformation. Sometimes, an early-adopting department or another company can set a good example or benchmark to follow.

+ Functional Reviews allow senior leaders to identify performance levels and opportunities across their division by requiring departments to report a standard set of measures in a structured presentation.

+ A formal program for change allows senior leaders to dedicate resources and focus to transforming to ETP. The formal program often includes both training of internal resources and coaching and apprenticeship to allow leaders to gain valuable experience in transforming teams and sustaining performance.

+ Process management and process maturity are complementary to an ETP deployment. ETP can also accompany a new technology system deployment or a change in location or sourcing (e.g., off-shoring of facilities to another country or out-sourcing of work to another company).

✦ Audits and ETP certification allow recognition of teams, departments, and leaders who are delivering the transformation and results.

✦ Senior leaders, just like the leaders of the departmental teams, have to learn to let their teams make their own decisions. After making the transformation, ETP teams need more support but less supervision.

Breakthrough: The Future of Engaged Team Performance

THROUGHOUT THIS BOOK, we've established that Engaged Team Performance will drive breakthroughs in business results for production teams. Hopefully by now you believe that premise and are thinking about ways to apply ETP at work. Go for it. But we'd also like to suggest that there may be other breakthroughs that could potentially be attained, particularly *where there are activities that are perceived as individual that would somehow benefit from a team approach.*

A More Personal Vision for ETP

Dodd drove downtown recently with his son James to pick up his prerace packet for the Atlanta Half-Marathon. After getting the bag of information, we passed over a test chip-reader gate, which I hadn't seen before. James's name popped up on a computer screen as we carried the packet over a bump on the floor. Back when I was 16, marathon runners didn't get microchips to tie to their shoes, but today that technology helps the race organizers keep track of everyone, prevents "shortcut" cheating, and automates the process of recording race times. As we pointed out at the beginning of the book, technology really is an amazing enabler of efficiency and effectiveness.

While we were driving back home, James and I were talking about the upcoming race, and he said he was already planning to run another one next year, the Birmingham Half Marathon, coming up in a few months. He said, "Hey, Dad, you've been doing some running lately; maybe you can run that one with me."

I casually said, "OK." Sometimes it seems too easy to *commit to change (Step 1),* and then you realize that you've got a lot of work to do to make it happen. You can always try to get out of the commitment, of course, but any parent of a 16-year-old will tell you that there aren't enough times that the kid wants to spend time with you, so you have to take what you can get. I decided that I was going to do it. After we got home, I took a look at the condition of my 40-year-old body in light of that recent commitment, and so I immediately got back in the car and went to the gym. It seems that many people make a similar commitment to physical fitness, and it's also possible that fitness commitments are some of the easiest to start and the toughest to follow through to finish. At least they are for me.

Our family has a membership at one of those large suburban mega-gyms. It's pretty nice. I went upstairs to the cardio area, a vast open bay with 200 machines in neat rows in front of a bank of televisions, and I saw 40 other people who were working out, each probably with some burning platform for change similar to mine. Or perhaps they were there because it was the day before Thanksgiving. Whatever; they were there.

Forty individuals working out individually. It seemed that something was missing.

Many sports are played as a team, of course. For those of you who played a competitive team sport as a child or young adult, you probably recall that the team practices resulted in some tough workouts. Having a team goal and some other team members there helped motivate everyone. If you learned to lift weights, you probably did that with a partner too; in addition to being available as a spotter, the partner helped to motivate you. It's hard to take a set off when your partner is standing there waiting to do his or her next set. The peer pressure keeps you working hard.

And then we become adults and go to work out by ourselves in a mega-gym in the midst of a large bank of cold, inhuman machines. No wonder I'm out of shape.

So, thinking about that, perhaps there's an opportunity to apply Engaged Team Performance concepts to adult physical fitness?

Some small-group fitness programs already use a team approach, for example with personal trainers leading a "boot camp" branded group workout; but that's often a premium service at the gym, so we'll try to apply the ETP concept more broadly.

We'll have to start by finding a way to *measure and analyze the process (Step 2)*, of course. As we investigate the current process and equipment at the gym, we quickly find that there are measurements everywhere. Each of those cardio machines collects immediate data from each person's workout, including distance, time, speed, work effort (in calories or watts), and even biological information like heart rate. The machines then promptly forget that information after each person's workout is finished.

So, what if the fitness center decided to install one of those marathon microchips inside each person's membership card and then networked the fitness machines wirelessly throughout the facility? The exercise machine could then capture live workout information, which could be saved as a secure personal record for each member on the fitness center's computer server.

This technology could certainly *streamline the work (Step 3)* for the person doing the exercising. If you work out on numerous machines (or worse, if you don't show up to the gym too often), you probably know how hard it is to remember all your levels and settings, which are different on each type of machine. Back when I took a weight-lifting class in college, the instructor even made us use paper cards to write down all the weight settings, repetitions, and set counts. We spent as much time taking notes as we spent lifting the weights. All of that could be automated if each machine could scan a member's card, identify the member, and download past workout data from a history file on the server. None of that would be technologically difficult.

Of course, the main benefit of the networked machines would be to *make the work and data visible (Step 4)*. Having access to trend data, perhaps from a Web site application, would allow fitness club members to watch and analyze their individual progress over time. The mega-gym has television screens everywhere, of course, and so workout data from individuals or teams could be displayed real time in the facility as people are exercising as well.

Oops, did we say workout data from "teams"? What if, with the new ways of collecting and displaying workout data, the fitness club finds some ways to *organize teams (Step 5)* of members? The club could offer random assignments to club members who wish to be placed onto teams that are competing with each other in certain categories (maybe calories burned or miles run per week). Perhaps the winning teams could win small prizes like T-shirts or have their members' names posted on one of those ubiquitous television screens? People will sometimes work harder for the team than they will work for their own personal benefit. Nobody wants to let the team down, even if the prize for winning is of nominal value or even just intangible recognition. The club would certainly have the information and ability to *set team goals (Step 6)* while still measuring the individual performance as well.

Ultimately, the approach would deliver measurable improvement in physical fitness results for the members, and it would probably be more fun too.

As they *lead the transition (Step 7)*, the club management would need to try some different variants of the team concepts, data collection types, and rewards and recognition mechanisms. With all these new processes and data linkages, the club could *sustain Engaged Team Performance (Step 8)* and demonstrate the value of the new approach over time.

The concept of *making a team goal out of an individual activity* helps both the individual and the team. You could think of more examples! Do any of you pay your kids for getting good grades? We do. It works sometimes. But perhaps if we set a *family* reward like a vacation to correspond with a team goal for the children combined, we might get better results with some collateral benefits of collaborative norms, like an eleventh grader helping an eighth grader study for a math test when the parents are unavailable. The eleventh grader probably understands the eighth grade math better than the parents do anyway! Families should be the ultimate teams. We really need to try that one.

For any of you who read the above ideas and don't buy into them yet, we recommend that you do three things:

1. Start to apply ETP in the workplace where teams are usually present but the members often perform instead as groups of individuals.

2. Go to the gym and work out with a partner and see how you feel afterward.

3. Think of some other, even better ways to apply the concepts in your life.

But regardless of how you decide to apply the concepts, we wish you all the best in your own journey to achieve game-changing results from Engaged Team Performance!

The GPS Case Study

This section repackages and elaborates upon content presented earlier in the book to provide a detailed summary of the Group Proposal Services team's journey to Engaged Team Performance.

Step 1. *Commit to Change*

It all started on the back of a napkin.

In 2006, a business leader in the specialty benefits division of the Principal Financial Group®, a large financial services firm, invited me to meet for lunch with a newly hired internal change agent. The business leader, Deb Blackman, was the director of Group Proposal Services (GPS), a sales support team that did quoting and proposals in support of the company's field distribution offices. I had been consulting for her company for a few years, teaching the typical Lean and Six Sigma process improvement tools and facilitating a couple of larger projects. And the change agent had just joined the company in a strategy director role, coming with strong process improvement credentials from General Electric (GE).

"Karsten Gebert, meet Dodd Starbird," she said. It was a key moment for all three of us.

The business leader had originally called the meeting to promote her strong vision for the organization learning to "manage with data" differently, and she pledged a willingness to experiment on her own team. She had been trying to get some traction for this idea for a while, and she was hoping that the strategy leader could drive the transformation and that our consulting company could help facilitate it. The strategy leader said that all he needed was a way to pay for the first project. So we did the typical "back of the napkin" sale on the table between our plates of Basil's pasta in the crowded restaurant:

"Tell me again, where do you think the opportunity is in your department?" I asked.

"We need better performance measures for efficiency," Deb explained. "I think our team is well led and motivated, and we have good processes, but we don't know how good we are. If we can measure this department well, then we can replicate that with less-efficient teams . . ."

"OK, just give me an idea of the kind of work you do . . . it's mostly quoting for sales proposals, right? So how many quotes does your team do per day?"

"Yes, we have a few peripheral things, but 95 percent of our work is quoting. Basically, we get a quote request by e-mail from the field office and create a proposal in the system. We do about 300 per day," she replied. I wrote "300" on the napkin.

Yes, there really was a napkin. We really wish we had kept it.

I continued, "So, give me an idea of how much work a quote takes; how much work time would you say it takes just to do one?"

This time she answered proudly, "We just did a time study on that—it's an average of 30 minutes for the main quoting work, maybe up to 35 including everyone who touches it." I wrote "300 units/day × 0.5 hour/unit = 150 hours/day" on the napkin.

Finally, I asked, "Tell me again, how many people did you say are in the department?"

Seeing the napkin and sensing now that there may have been a greater opportunity than she had originally thought, she replied, "There are *65*. But 11 of those 65 are temps."

"Thanks for telling us all of that. And I know it's a little scary to let us play with your real numbers here. But remind me, have I ever told you about the *magic equation* for a transactional process like yours . . . ?"

The two of us had known each other for a long time, and so the conversation was more candid than many similar ones turn out to be. She knew immediately where the conversation was headed after she looked down at the napkin.

Conceptually: *work time* × *volume* = *people*
(but in reality, it never does!)

So of course, 150 hours work time per day should take only *30* people working 5 hours a day, which is a good fully loaded assumption for a day's work that includes vacation, personal time off, meetings, etc. Even with the typical "overhead" of supervisors, trainers, and quality inspectors (which turned out to be 8 people), they were overstaffed.

The business leader, to her great credit, quickly accepted the high-level assessment as a real opportunity rather than an indictment of her leadership team. She knew the effort might expose her team to scrutiny in the short term, but she trusted that the results would make the team look good in the long term. (And sure enough, two years later, the GPS workplace was the most toured and benchmarked area in the division.)

I reassured her that this kind of opportunity really is typical for many businesses and departments that we initially assess, and it was fortunately all too believable for the strategy leader, who said, "Don't worry; it feels like a project here will quickly pay for itself. If it doesn't, I'll cover it somehow from my own budget. I'll make that commitment. When can you get started?"

Discussion Questions

+ Is inefficiency alone a sufficiently compelling reason to achieve Step 1 of ETP (*commit to change*)?

+ Is this leader's reaction to the calculation unusual? How could she have reacted?

+ What else would you have asked the leadership team to assess regarding the need to transform the team's process and performance?

+ What enabled the conversation to be so candid?

+ How do you imagine that customers felt about the team's performance? Is there any way to know without asking them?

Step 2. *Measure and Analyze the Process*

The GPS department creates quotes for group health, dental, life, and disability products. The department receives approximately 300 requests for quotes daily from its partners in the field sales force. In 2006, the expected turnaround time (TAT) for producing a quote was 48 hours, and in normal situations the team was able to meet that goal 80 to 95 percent of the time, depending on volumes.

In the prior year's "busy season" of 2005 (September–November), however, the team had experienced a drop in its service levels, missing the TAT goal consistently, which was attributed by leaders at the time to the fact that volumes had exceeded the team's capacity. The leaders wanted to ensure that 2006 turned out better.

Knowing they needed to include the team members in designing the new process, the department leaders identified an internal project leader, three assistant managers, and a number of Sales Support Specialists (SSSs) to form a team. In the initial team meeting, we facilitated a visioning exercise that invoked the principles of Lean flow. Some of the thoughts on the flip chart were:

+ "Once & Done" processing (no repeat touch)
+ No redundant work; minimum touch
+ "Do It Right the First Time"
+ Capacity matched to demand
+ Rational handoffs versus specialization (hand off only when we have to)
+ Workforce engagement
+ Scalable to demand and variation
+ Team measures, goals, and accountabilities

All those things seemed reasonable, but nobody was sure how *possible* they were. So even though many of the team members knew the process by heart, they agreed to make a high-level process map called a SIPOC (an acronym that stands for "suppliers-inputs-process-outputs-customers") and then job-shadow real SSSs to watch the process in action.

At a high level, the process was:

+ The GPS department created quotes for group health, dental, life, and disability products.

+ GPS received approximately 300 requests for quotes daily from its partners in the field sales force, and it returned the quotes to those partners within 48 hours (a key customer requirement).

+ When the requests for quote (RFQs) were received, they were printed and inspected to decide if they were "rush" or "standard" requests. Standard requests went to a queue for processing the next day ("tomorrow's work"), and rush requests were sent for immediate processing.

+ A specialist (SSS) then "prepped" a batch of quotes, by looking up some key information (e.g., demographics of the new prospective customer).

+ Next, another specialist reviewed the RFQ and created a "prep sheet" for data entry, using a word processor template that was designed to capture the appropriate information that would need to be entered into the system.

+ The prep sheets went into a queue for Consolidated Data Entry team members ("CDEs"—usually temporary employees) to enter into the company's computer-generated proposal system.

+ The CDE then placed the completed quote in an electronic folder for the field office to retrieve, and sent an e-mail to tell the GPS department that the entry had been completed, attaching any important notes that the department needed to know.

+ After the quote was entered into the system, the paperwork was sent to "Post Tracking" (another group of temporary employees), who tracked the quote and some pertinent performance information that the department needed (turnaround time, etc.) in another database called "Full Service Log."

Like many processes, there were a number of steps with hand-offs to different people, and there were quite a few acronyms, tools, and systems in use in the department! As you probably know from your own company, that's typical too.

The next step was to look at the customer requirements to make sure the process was designed for success. Obviously, the customers wanted their quotes to be timely, accurate, and complete. They seemed happy with the 48-hour turnaround standard, though there were some anecdotal issues about "quality" that were somewhat disputed.

Like most good departments, GPS regularly solicited feedback from customers in the field, and it kept track of complaints and issues as it resolved them. The Pareto chart in Figure A-1 shows some of the complaints that GPS had received lately and had internally categorized. The department was not sure that every issue was being reported, but 160 complaints out of thousands of quotes wasn't too bad. The team had a passionate discussion of the "read your mind" error, which seemed to mean that the field

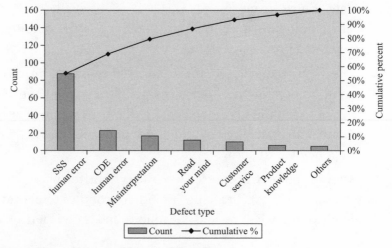

Figure A-1   Pareto Chart of Feedback

offices believed that GPS should know certain preferences without being told, and one person explained that every field office wanted it to be Burger King (from the old commercial, "Have it your way...").

GPS had previously created a "benefit map" to capture the different preferences for each sales rep and field office, and the expectation was that the SSS would know the office's preferences and apply them appropriately—for example, even if a broker (the field office's customer) had specified only certain provisions in the request for quote, the SSS was expected to know if, when, and how to apply the field office's preferences to provide additional information that the broker hadn't specified. It seemed quite complicated! Hence, the SSS team members were convinced that only one person could service each field office effectively.

There was also a general opinion that "reducing and standardizing the options offered" to the customer would allow better sharing of work. When someone referred to this idea as making "vanilla quotes," the department leader seemed very displeased. But the Lean Six Sigma approach very clearly encourages people to understand and try to *meet* customers' needs, not start by trying to negotiate them down; and so after some offline recalibration within the leadership team, the project team continued along with the general agreement that the team would need to try to maintain the policy of meeting the individual preferences of each field office. The project team also decided to measure the impact of those preferences before trying to make a decision.

Drawing from both the Lean and Six Sigma methodologies, the team needed to measure both the process flow (using a Lean tool called a Value Stream Map) and the inherent variation in the process (a core Six Sigma concept).

The Value Stream Map (VSM) is shown in Figure A-2. The VSM takes a traditional process map and adds critical information about the process directly to it, creating a single visual

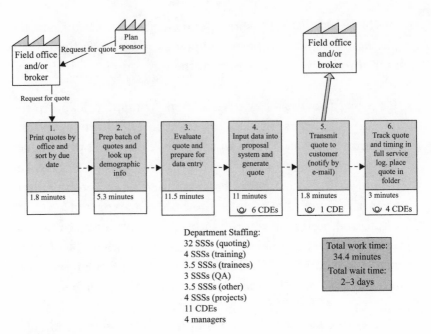

Figure A-2 Produce Quotes

picture of the process that can be quite useful for analysis. Some of the typical information types are:

+ Value of each process step
+ Staffing for each process step
+ Volume flow rate of customer demand for products or services
+ Work time to do each step
+ Work in process (inventory) waiting (and wait time) before each step
+ Information flow to control work

After gathering a plethora of data, the team needed to apply both process and data analysis techniques to understand the reasons for the current state of the process.

A quick study of the previous month's quote volume showed some interesting daily variation. Obviously, with a required two-day turnaround time, the team couldn't be sized for the average volume, since some days were much heavier than others. The daily variation looked as it does in Figure A-3. The volume charts show that the average daily volume was 311, but the typical expected range of potential daily volumes (about 3 standard deviations) was +/−100!

While we won't discuss every data chart that the GPS team produced and analyzed, we will highlight one more critical piece of information: work time. The GPS team had actually already done a time study before the project started. The team had gathered both the work time and the attributes of individual quotes, which allowed the project team to calculate the average time for the SSSs and data entry CDEs to do the main work in processing a quote: 29.6 minutes, just as the department leader had said from the beginning.

The team quickly collected data from the other players in the process—for example, the CDEs doing printing and tracking tasks. All of it made it onto the Value Stream Map. The team members had some great conversations along the way as they created the VSM. To paraphrase some highlights:

"Prepping is helping without really helping," one of the specialists said. She was referring to Step 2, the way that some SSSs would try to help another team member who was swamped. Because they didn't know the other person's office preferences, they couldn't help by doing a whole quote. But they could do

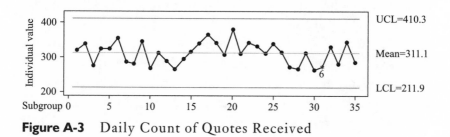

Figure A-3   Daily Count of Quotes Received

some of the menial demographic data lookup work at the beginning of the quoting task.

It turned out that the help didn't really help, due to a behavioral and accountability issue. "Yeah, I have to admit that I check the information anyway, after someone preps for me," another SSS replied. "After all, the quote has my name on it, so it's me who would get in trouble if it's wrong." It sounded like the prepping step was redundant.

"But what else could we help with? It's all because of the differences in the office preferences and benefit maps. If the offices would just standardize what they want, we'd be able to help each other with complete quotes, but it's so hard to learn each office's preferences that prepping is the only way we can help each other." Back to vanilla quotes again . . .

This conversation revealed that the preferences were actually *all already written down.* Each office had submitted a preference template with all of its preferences listed. So the project team decided to just measure the feared effect of having to learn a new office's preferences. The team gave a "benefit map" from a specific field office to an SSS who didn't support that office, and the team timed her while she did some quotes. The first few took 5 to 10 minutes longer than normal. After that, she did them almost as fast as that office's regular SSS. The team realized that it was potentially painful and stressful to cross-train, perhaps, but certainly not impossible.

Another fairly obvious handoff problem had a more insidious cause. "What about the CDEs and the data entry?" another person asked. "That template that the SSS fills out has exactly the same information as the proposal system that the CDEs use; why didn't we just have the SSS enter it into the system directly and skip the CDE altogether?"

"Oh, there was a good reason for that . . . [There always is!] Originally, the computer proposal system was underpowered and very slow. It didn't make sense for an expensive resource like the SSS to be tied up waiting for screens to update during data entry. And when we ran into capacity issues last fall, we found that we could hire temps and teach them the proposal system pretty quickly, whereas it's hard to teach SSSs their whole job—they really have to know a lot about products. So with the CDEs we could more quickly react to volume changes." They had missed the obvious point that the CDE was doing a completely redundant role, now that the system speed issue had been fixed.

But that brought up another question: "What happened last fall anyway?"

"Well, our volumes increased dramatically, and we got behind. Like all organizations, we occasionally have some attrition, and we were in the midst of training some new people we had hired to replace some experienced people who had moved on to other roles in the company. Our people get promotions into other departments partly because the SSS role is such a great place to learn the company's product line. Then when new folks are in training, we have to check 100 percent of their work, which takes extra time."

A measurement of the actual volumes quickly verified that the dramatic "50 percent volume spike" was a bit of an urban legend. The volume increase during the last busy season had been about 10 percent, the same as that of the two previous years. It was true that they'd gotten behind, but it had been caused by the capacity constraints due to the normal attrition and training issues that had just happened at the wrong time, right before the busy season. When capacity doesn't meet demand, a team can get behind fast. And then it takes even more work to keep up once the "Where's my quote?" phone call questions start coming in.

The members of the team felt bad about their past issues, and they were truly dedicated to having a better busy season in the coming fall. They finished the Analyze phase with some good ideas.

Discussion Questions

+ Why bring together a team to solve this—isn't the solution obvious? Discuss the ways that teams help to expose issues by sharing information, challenging paradigms, and brainstorming ideas.

+ Why did they start with a SIPOC map when everyone on the team already knows the high-level process?

+ Not all components of a VSM are used in the story—discuss whether you believe teams should use process improvement tools the "right way" or make adjustments based on the situation.

+ While every business has different processes, and hence will need some measures to be tailored to the specific situation, what are the "typical measures" that should be collected for *every* ETP effort?

+ Why do businesses have processes that don't work efficiently or effectively? There are usually some good reasons . . . list some of them.

+ Are all handoffs bad? What are some good reasons to put a handoff in a process?

+ Are all leaders brave enough to undertake an ETP effort? How is the leader perceived when the team finds substantial opportunities to improve?

Step 3. *Streamline the Work*

The process changes that the team implemented were fairly obvious and straightforward. Basically, the team cut out all the handoffs and had the SSSs do the entire quote from start to finish and then track their own data in the tracking database. This meant that the SSS team would have to be trained on using the proposal-generating system for data entry and also the tracking system (Full Service Log). A few team members reluctantly volunteered to try it, and by the following week they decided that they never wanted to go back to the old process. The new way was much faster.

To continue to prove the concept, the project team enlisted the support of the existing Midwest team to pilot the changes.

Six team members, many who had participated in the project team's analysis meetings as well, were trained on the systems and began to process quotes the new way. The new process had fewer steps, as shown in Figure A-4.

We shouldn't minimize the effort that it took to pilot the process with the Midwest team, make small changes to the plan, and then cross-train and reorganize an entire department over a whole summer. It was a Herculean task, and the GPS team had its ups and downs but stayed focused on being ready for the busy season in the fall.

The team hit that busy season with 11 fewer people (after the temporary employees in CDE roles were redeployed elsewhere) and had no service or backlog issues during the next busy season. The project was a smashing success. The field offices noticed that their quotes were being returned much faster, and they also saw fewer errors, which was another consequence of the reduction of handoffs. The people had worked very hard to change, and many of them later said that the summer was a very difficult time, but they'd do it again in a heartbeat.

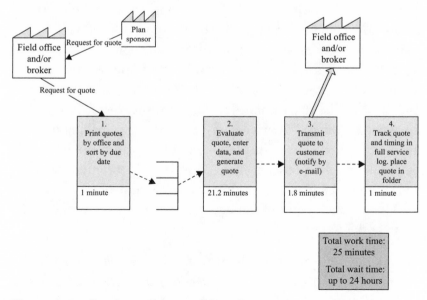

Figure A-4   Produce Quotes (New Process)

Discussion Questions

+ What are the "design principles"—the attributes of a good process—that create a vision to help the team identify how to redesign the process?

+ Some of the design principles are counterintuitive (e.g., why allow a more expensive resource to do a less expensive job just to avoid a handoff?)—discuss.

+ How long should you run a pilot? Why and how would that vary in different situations?

+ What challenges do you imagine that the team experienced in deploying the extensive process changes?

+ What would you have done differently in changing the GPS processes?

Step 4. *Make the Work and Data Visible*

One of the key differences in delivering upon the promise of Engaged Team Performance lies in the approach and vigor dedicated to implementing visual work and data controls.

Like too many teams do, the GPS team almost lost its way on the path to the Control phase. It started out with the best of intentions. The department leader, from the very beginning of the project, wanted to drive data-based decision making into the team's culture. So even as the project team was in the middle of implementing the process changes during the summer, the leaders scheduled a planning session to discuss control measures.

Here is an excerpt of the department leader's message to the team at the time:

... I do have an expectation that certain topics will be addressed during the day and that one or more of you will be on-point for specific topics ...

✦ *Be prepared with the straw-man control charts or at least the current state. When Dodd visited with us briefly about control mechanisms, he had provided a template regarding components of control charts (source, reason for control, etc.). In addition, I would like to see some preliminary results.*

✦ *Please be prepared regarding any current or planned changes and your expectation around the quality/training component of the GPS process.*

✦ *Be prepared with an updated understanding of any project milestones or challenges.*

You've all done a super job in executing some big changes; let's get this last piece of Control nailed. This, to me, is the most exciting part of all (and not because it's the numbers stuff). This is what makes the process sustainable and what makes the improvements a way of life.

She was dead-on right, and her vision for sustainable performance measurement was critical to their later success. But for all the great intentions, the team almost didn't get there.

After a great planning session in the summer, the team was asked to create a package of data charts and begin to post them in the team areas. The department leader scheduled one more follow-up meeting on September 26 to showcase the measures and the new process. She invited a number of her peers—other department leaders in the company who were interested in engaging in similar process improvement efforts and emplacing similar controls. It was intended as a victory tour.

As we started to walk through the facility, the group came around the corner into a team area and found the team's data board. There were no data charts, and there was a single message on it, "Team 3 Rocks!"

The department leader was quite unhappy and a bit embarrassed by the missing charts and the slogan scrawled on the data board that day, but she realized that it would just take a bit more work to get it done. Yet the "Team 3 Rocks!" slogan actually became a rallying cry to finish the Control phase work.

The team had plenty of good reasons for the initial failure: the process changes, a facility move, and the preparations for the September-to-November busy season had all seemed more important. The team had already gotten the gains from the process changes when it redeployed the 11 temporary CDE employees earlier in the summer. And so the data had seemed to be a longer-term priority.

The department leader stuck to her vision, however, and she made a very clear statement by immediately reassigning one of the three supervisors to be a full-time data analyst to support the Control phase effort. Finally realizing that she was serious about the importance of the data charts, the department teams put the charts up and started using them.

It sounds so simple, but it really took weeks of work to identify the right ways to measure the team's process, inputs, and outputs and then set up the system linkages, reports, and analytical tools so that the numbers could be updated and reprinted for display every morning.

Ultimately, the access to the data allowed the team to establish the right team performance measures and goals. *Engaged Team Performance can't work without data,* and no team we've ever met has had the right data when it started its ETP journey. There is *always* work to be done to establish solid control measures.

Effectiveness Measures

The Group Proposal Services department had a number of customer-facing measures, particularly a customer satisfaction survey, a complaint tracking system, and a regularly reviewed turnaround time measure, which the department called TAT. In 2006, GPS had only existed for a couple of years, and the customer satisfaction scores had always been substantially less than desired.

As the GPS team members prepared their dashboard of measures for their teams to monitor performance, they added complaints and customer satisfaction ratings on time-ordered charts.

Though it might seem that 80 percent human error is primarily a "people problem," the performance actually got much better when the department implemented its process changes. Taking out three handoffs and having a single person complete each quote from start to finish helped to minimize the effects of misinterpretation, handwriting issues, and dispersed accountability. Complaint rates declined dramatically, and satisfaction improved.

Efficiency Measures

The turnaround time issue, however, took a different kind of approach to fix. In reality, TAT was a measure of effectiveness that was *driven by efficiency.* A process with three handoffs takes longer to get the same work done because the item going through it (the quote) has to sit in three work queues for three different people. When you hear a person proudly state, "I work on everything I get within 24 hours of when I received it," that sounds great until you realize that three of those people in a row would guarantee 2 to 3 days of waiting time to get a 30-minute quote done. That was exactly the challenge.

When the GPS project started, the department was measuring TAT as "percent of quotes completed within 48 hours of receipt." A good TAT was considered 95 percent, but the department rarely hit that goal, and during the busy season it had been more like 80 percent. At the end of the project, the department was measuring TAT in hours, looking at the typical (average) TAT as well as the variation (moving range). And after implementing the process changes, the vast majority of quotes were completed within 24 hours.

In order to monitor and display team and individual efficiency, the team needed to know:

+ Who accomplished which tasks on what day ("completion volumes")
+ How long each task was expected to take ("standard time")
+ How long each person was scheduled to be doing "production" tasks
+ How long each person was paid to be working

The time study that had been accomplished during the process analysis phase gave the team plenty of data on the standard times, and a regression analysis enabled the team to understand the variation in the work well enough to give fair credit for the inherent variation from quote to quote, which was a key factor in being able to predict the *standard work time* that each task should take.

As the GPS department refined its work controls, it created charts to compare actual team performance (from self-reported task timing) with the standard time expected by the equations. Basically, the department created a computer program to feed system information about completed quotes into a spreadsheet, which then applied the coefficients from the regression equation to predict the work time for each quote. A GPS systems analyst linked the spreadsheet to graphs that compared predicted work time for each quote with the actual reported time, with the ability to measure at both a team and an individual level.

The analyst started with the team chart in Figure A-5, so that each team could compare its actual daily performance with the standard time expected by the regression equation. At an aggregate level, an equation's average predictions are quite accurate. You can see how close the team results matched the expected

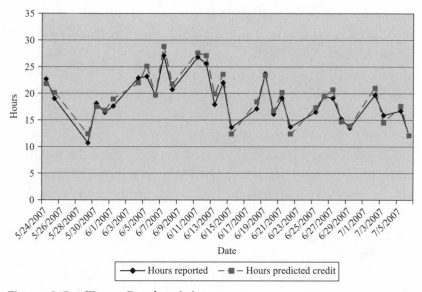

Figure A-5   Team Productivity

work time each day; this chart actually gave both the leaders and the teams great confidence that the process was being measured and predicted accurately. When the lines diverged as a trend for more than a few days, there was always an explainable cause; a new team member in training would cause a three- to four-week upward shift in the team's actual hours (higher than the standard time) until the person got comfortable with the product knowledge, process, and office preferences and began performing at a similar speed to that of the other team members.

Leaders and team members could clearly see how each team was performing.

Measuring Engaged Team Performance always starts with measuring the *team*. But eventually, the leaders in the GPS department also created individual charts to share monthly with each team member. The variation in day-to-day quoting time was high enough that the individual charts weren't useful to judge daily individual performance, but they were quite accurate over the interval of a month to compare a person's actual work time with the standard. Figure A-6 shows a recent example of an individual's monthly data.

Each person gets feedback on his or her predicted work completion credit compared with self-reported time. In Figure A-6, this SSS is right on her predicted time (the bottom two lines almost match). The Hours Available measure (top line) is the amount of time that the person was paid to be in the building, while the Quoting Process time (second from the top line) allows comparison of time credit with the amount of time that the person was assigned to be doing production work. All in all, these measures let people know exactly how they are doing, and the end-of-year performance evaluation is never a surprise.

Best of all, because the predicted times match the actual times so closely in aggregate, the team members all have confidence that they are being measured fairly. Hard work can

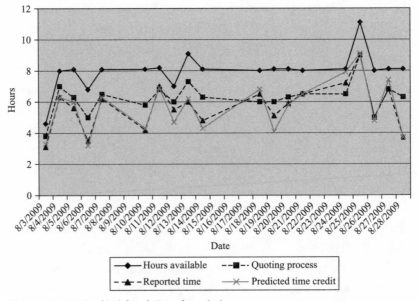

Figure A-6 Individual Productivity

be recognized, and coasting is easy to identify. The team likes the measurements; people are OK with being measured when the measures are fair.

Integrating Visual Measures and Visual Work

One of the key challenges of driving Engaged Team Performance is that the process and measurements are highly interdependent, and so a change in one necessitates a change in both. Thus, as we deployed both sets of changes, the GPS team had to redesign its work area to facilitate the integration of the new processes and measurements.

As we've already illustrated, the most important team goal in the GPS department was the one about getting all the work done for the customer, regardless of which individual on the team did it. To assist the team in *seeing* that performance, the leaders made some changes to the work area to enable *visual control*. Visual control is a key concept of Lean Enterprise that encourages workflow, status, and problems to be visually obvious. Anyone who walks into the work area should be able to ascertain how well the team is doing just by looking around.

Prior to the improvement project at GPS, each Sales Support Specialist kept the requests for quotes on an electronic list, composed of e-mails in an Outlook folder. Every day, each SSS would print a batch of requests and keep the stack of papers on his or her desk. If there were leftover requests at night, those would need to be locked up since they had privacy-controlled data on them. The work was hidden in desks and computers, with no way to see how much was there. Every morning, the team leader would hold a meeting to ask if anyone needed help, and each SSS would update a whiteboard with count data about the inventory of requests, sorted by age in days. The leader and the team would have a similar recap near the middle of the day to recalibrate, again trying to shift resources if needed. Like a stopped clock, the numbers were right twice per day! All the rest of the time, nobody really knew how the team was doing overall in meeting the customers' turnaround time requirements.

To change the team's perception of the timeliness goal and increase its awareness of performance, the pilot team first changed its seating arrangement. Rather than having desks in cubicles in separate rows, the pilot team moved to an open "cell" structure, with all team members' cubicle walls lowered and the desks facing inward toward the team's center so that the members of the team could communicate and collaborate. The whiteboard with the performance data went onto a table in the middle, as did a new tool: a stack of trays. Instead of hiding the work in and around individuals' desks, the new process required the quote requests to reside in trays, one three-tray set for each field office, with the top tray for rush orders (due today) and the two trays below that for quotes due on the following days. At any moment, any team member could look at the trays and identify how well the whole team was doing. From the location and thickness of the stacks of paper, everyone could see which offices needed immediate support in order to meet the team's goal. Every night, the work in the bottom trays was moved up one tray higher, and the process started again the next day. The work was now visible.

The team also needed the *data* to be visible. During the pilot of the new process, the team had to briefly create a new role to control the workflow and reporting system. One volunteer, who turned out to be a great contributor and peer leader for the department, became a "simulated computer program" to manually gather information and display it for the team. Her main role was to count the work-in-process inventory in each bin every two hours and post the updated information on the whiteboard. She also printed the quote requests, put them in the trays, and counted all the work as it was completed. It was a tough job for her because she would have preferred to spend all her time doing "real" work, but the team needed to measure the performance in order to understand the process capacity. Later, after the process design was validated and the team was comfortable with the setup, most of those tasks were automated by the information technology group; the status reports and efficiency charts could be printed on demand. The lesson for the team was that sometimes the benefits of visual control and measurement are worth a little bit of extra-yet-temporary work.

Discussion Questions

+ What is the difference between efficiency and effectiveness measures?

+ Explain the relationship between the "magic equation" in Step 1 and the method for calculating efficiency in Step 4. How does the gap between work done and time paid on the chart in Figure A-6 relate to the assumption of "five hours work in an eight-hour day"?

+ A regression equation is complex to create and use for prediction of work time. Why was it important in this case?

+ Why the push for daily and real-time data; why isn't a monthly report sufficient?

+ We do quite a bit of work collecting and posting data—why is this a valuable investment of time?

+ Why is a control chart specified? What are the key attributes of a control chart?

+ Why would you do steps 1 through 4 first before trying to automate the process (through a new information system)?

Step 5. *Organize the Team*

For most processes, once the team has a reliable understanding of standard work time, the leaders can create a bottom-up staffing model. Of course, every leader in every business in the world already has a staffing model, but most of those are top down. That might not seem to be such a big deal, but it's actually a critical difference. We'll explain ...

A top-down model is based on past history of a department's size and its volume. Often filled with multiple complex-looking calculations of volume mix, absenteeism assumptions, and performance adjustment factors, those models are inherently based on the assumption that if volume increases by 10 percent, staffing should increase by 10 percent.

The bottom-up staffing model starts from the work, calculating the number of people needed to crew the team based upon the volume of work, the standard work time, and certain assumptions of availability of people, based for instance on the amount of vacation that the company offers, the tenure of the team, and current attendance rates. Most of our models expect people to be working about five hours per paid eight-hour day. Reminds you of the magic equation that we introduced earlier, doesn't it? It's the same concept.

The GPS team actually calculated the work time and staffing numbers to support its new team concept using real historical volume data from the prior year. The team tried various configurations and combinations of field offices until it was able to divide the department into six equal-sized teams. It gathered system data about the attributes of actual quotes to feed into the regression equations, predicting the amount of work that each team would have needed to do each day, week, and month. It also looked at daily variation and designed the teams' sizes to handle the *average plus one standard deviation* of daily volume during the peak time period, with additional capacity for the rare heavy day to come from assistance from other teams or from overtime. Below is the final staffing model, which the team tested for both typical and "peak" expected volumes:

Team	1	2	3	4	5	6
Average work time/day (Aug–Mar)	838	1,103	1,421	1,022	1,476	1,307
Standard deviation/day	288	284	438	358	488	405
Recent Volumes						
Average work time/day (Feb–Mar)	907	1,132	1,559	1,047	1,514	1,361
Standard deviation/day	249	233	337	293	415	357
AVG + 1 STDEV =	1,156	1,364	1,897	1,340	1,929	1,718
Staffing at 5-hour days (FTE)	3.9	4.5	6.3	4.5	6.4	5.7
Recommended staffing:	5	5	6	5	7	6
Peak 2005 Volumes						
Average work time/day (Sep–Nov 2005)	895	1,121	1,503	1,113	1,652	1,433
Standard deviation/day	301	243	425	366	463	395
AVG + 1 STDEV =	1,196	1,365	1,928	1,479	2,116	1,828
Staffing at 5-hour days (FTE)	4.0	4.5	6.4	4.9	7.1	6.1
Recommended staffing	5	5	7	6	7	6

The numbers showed that Team 3 would need an additional person during the busy season, which could come from the training department since training would be curtailed during those three months. The team had a great plan!

At the time, nobody believed that the department could do the work with only 36 people (the bottom row of the chart shows the final team sizes, which add up to 36). In the first busy season after the project was implemented, the department actually had quite a few more people than that available. Over time, through teamwork and performance management, the department gained confidence that this staffing model was actually right. Two years later, after attrition of employees who weren't replaced, the department was down to 38 people, including leadership and support.

Discussion Questions

+ Have you ever tried to reorganize a team *without* doing the process analysis and bottom-up staffing efficiency data collection that GPS did? What did happen or would have happened?

+ Discuss ways to present and manage the change in staffing requirements from an ETP effort.

+ When you heard the "magic equation story" in Step 1, did you believe that the team would actually get down to the staffing level that the napkin predicted?

+ What additional concerns would you have if this had been a collective bargaining (union) shop? How would you engage the employees in supporting the potential changes?

Step 6. Set Team Goals

At the beginning of the GPS project, the department managers had a daily performance tracking system in place (good!) that was based on keeping counts of each person's "quotes done per day" (bad!). At first glance, it seems to be the right way to measure things, but it drives the wrong behaviors. In this case, the magic number was 15.

Each person was expected to complete 15 quotes per day. The performance goal had been set based on observations of fully qualified specialists over the last couple of years, and in general it wasn't far from wrong. But the problems with the measurement became obvious once the team did some statistical analysis of the initial time study.

The analysis started with some simple internal benchmarking. There was one Sales Support Specialist in the department whom the leaders singled out as by far the fastest quote generator. Instead of the expected 15 quotes per day, she was able to crank out an average of 18 per day. We went to see her first.

She seemed almost embarrassed about her greatness, and over and over she claimed that she wasn't doing anything special or different. She didn't mean to be faster than the other team members, and she was worried about all the attention. She couldn't identify any causes. Her manager said, "She's just a really hard worker." Perhaps she was even considering slowing down so that all the attention would go away.

Some of the variation in individual results in GPS was caused by differences in the quotes themselves, not the performance of the people. But the individual goal was still 15 quotes per day—and everyone thought the goal was right, even though it wasn't delivering much value in motivating anyone.

As we proceeded with the GPS project, we found that the time to make a quote was a function of a number of things, and we demonstrated statistically that 75 percent of the variation in work time was driven by concrete factors specific to each quote. Therefore, individual effort was worth at most 25 percent (and probably a lot less).

As they progressed through the project, the team members were able to gather system data on the quotes that everyone in the department had completed in the last month and then run them through the calculation to determine how much "time credit" each person had earned. And—surprise, surprise!—the fastest person wasn't really the fastest! She was actually getting a slightly higher share of smaller and simpler quotes from the field office she supported. She was right that she wasn't doing anything different. In fact, she was exactly average. There were some other folks, however, who had been struggling to get their 15 quotes per day and were found to be doing more than their share of harder quotes. The equation helped the leadership team see that setting a volume-based goal of 15 quotes per day was both unfair *and* unwise.

The concept of *tomorrow's work* came from a behavior that the GPS team members adopted to ensure that they always met the individual goals. The logic was something like:

+ Something that arrives today is not "due" until two days from now.

+ As a Sales Support Specialist, I have to do 15 quotes per day (my goal).

+ Due to the inherent variation in incoming volume, I'm not sure how many quotes will come in tomorrow from the field office I support (sometimes it's even zero!).

+ Since I only usually do work for this one field office, I have to save 15 of its quotes to do tomorrow, or I will definitely fail to make my goal tomorrow.

+ Therefore, anything that comes in today is tomorrow's work, and I'm probably also going to stop today (or find something else to do) after I finish 15 quotes, so that I can make sure that I have enough to do tomorrow.

The project team confirmed the impact of the goal on individual behaviors by monitoring the process directly for a few days and observing that people who had met their daily goal by the early afternoon would often stop doing quotes and start working on other tasks (training, special projects, answering e-mails, etc.). As we suspected, not only was the 15-per-day goal failing to drive productivity; it was actually *reducing* productivity!

The individual goal distracted the people from the real team goal, which, of course, should have been to *get perfect quotes back to every customer on time*. Because defect-free quotes with a smile are nonnegotiable (those results should still be measured, of course, but the goal is perfection), the turnaround time was really the only team measurement that needed to be treated as a goal. But it needed to be a *team* goal, not an individual one, particularly because of the variation in incoming volume. Sometimes a team member didn't have enough work from his or her assigned field office and really should have done some of the quotes from another team member's office. But that didn't happen because there was a perception that it was too hard to learn another office's preferences. Ultimately, with individuals only accountable to deliver a certain number of quotes per day, the only person whose goals were really tied to the customer's experience was the manager, and that's a very bad deal for the manager.

So the GPS team created a simple goal for the teams: *get all quotes back to the customer, done right, within 24 hours of arrival.* Each team measured those results—turnaround time in hours, with quality scores—on a white dry-erase board, along with trend charts with other predictors (also called "leading indicators") such as incoming volumes, current work-in-process inventories, and cross-training status. Teams that were within goal timing were constantly recognized, and small incentives such as pizza parties were occasionally awarded as well. These incentives were team incentives, of course, with all team members sharing in the recognition for meeting the team goals.

The GPS team also used a team incentive of "blue jeans weeks" for teams that were going through the extra work to pilot the new process. Suspending the company's dress code policies for teams that were performing to expectations during the pilot phase turned out to be the most motivating team reward. The employees appreciated the relaxed environment as they were learning new processes and trying to reduce cycle-time results for the customers. It was a win-win; the incentive didn't cost the company anything, and the employees valued it.

Before they implemented ETP, the members of the team really hadn't been acting like a team. They were just a group of people supervised by the same manager. A team works together. These folks just worked in the same location as individuals . . . *In order to achieve Engaged Team Performance, the entire GPS department first needed to come together behind a team goal.*

As the GPS teams began to accept the new vision (perfect quotes delivered 30 minutes after receipt) and the new team goal (reducing cycle time to under 24 hours), they found that the collaborative norms supported the metrics and the team goal because everyone was focused on the same thing. The visual controls told the team members what work needed to happen, and they collaborated to make decisions on the fly about which work tray each of them would pull a request from next. The team was beginning to become engaged!

Discussion Questions

+ Why is it important to size the team for the right capacity before trying to set a team goal? What would happen if the team is undersized? Or if it is too large?

+ Are team goals enough to drive performance, or do you still need to measure individual performance?

+ If you do measure individual performance, how do you ensure each person performs appropriately without setting an *individual goal* that will have adverse effects? How can you determine what the standards should be?

+ What are the differences between a "group of individuals" and a "team"?

+ Will all the original personnel support the changes that ETP drives in measurement and metrics? What happens to those who don't?

+ In this case "blue jeans week" was a simple, free reward for the team—can you think of others?

+ What complexities would remote workers add to this "team" construct?

Step 7. *Lead the Transition*

Although many associates were kept in the same team(s) or were supporting the same offices, there were some people who had to learn new office preferences, and then the teams needed to accomplish the cross-training plan before the busy season hit. The GPS team was able to plan to phase the team changes and training over the summer months. The cross-training turned out to be a lot of work, and each team had to be adequately trained before it could make the jump to the work-sharing norms that were required.

This was reorganization the right way: the reorganization of the work, process, and metrics led to a planned, purposeful, and well-timed reorganization of the team. Anyone who has survived a reorganization taking the opposite approach will recognize the difference. The wrong way to reorganize starts with a secret meeting to discuss "who's going to lead what group" and eventually ends in a brief discussion of "what does each group do." In contrast, the GPS reorganization was actually remembered by the team members as a tough experience with a very positive outcome! We were able to interview a panel of GPS team members at a training event the following year, and they confirmed that it was hard work to make the changes, but they'd never want to go back to the way the process and the organization were before.

The department leaders initially ran and then occasionally updated a staffing analysis for each team, using the regression model to predict the amount of work time using actual quote volumes (both from a recent time period and from the previous busy season). They then recalculated the necessary staffing levels and adjusted the team composition and office assignments accordingly. This staffing model precisely balanced capacity and demand for each team. The analysis was done monthly during the transition, and then the department reassessed it quarterly to ensure that each team maintained the proper resources and capacity to meet its current and future expected demand.

The cycle time came down and the work efficiency came up as the changes took hold. As turnover happened on the teams, unfilled positions were not replaced if they were no longer needed. Eventually, the teams were working at their true capacity.

The field offices started to notice the change in performance effectiveness quickly. The vice president of field operations, Jenifer Moses, says, "The company had made changes to GPS before, but we had always changed standards and volume mix instead of changing the way we did the work. After this change, we immediately noticed a dramatic improvement in timing. The real 'tell' was when some of the most vocal field sales reps started using the GPS to do more of their quotes."

Cindy Close, one of Jenifer's team members, adds, "There was a change in timing, of course, but the difference in quality was just as important to us as the timing." And that feedback was based on reductions in complaints and cycle time; the field offices didn't know at the time that the transformation also came with a labor cost savings of $1.2 million per year as well. Cindy says, "At some companies, the field might see a home office cost reduction as a possible indicator of reduced service levels, but this was the opposite. Costs and service both improved. It was a win-win."

The key to completing the transformation to Engaged Team Performance lies in completely *integrating* processes, measures, team goals, visual work, collaborative norms, and organization. It's hard work both for leaders and for their teams, and sometimes it can take months or even years to accomplish.

Discussion Questions

+ How long could it take to lead the transition?

+ What details and preparation work would be necessary before the team can "pull the trigger" and move to the final organizational design?

+ Have you ever been on a team that was forced to make the jump with an organizational change without figuring out all those details first? How did that feel?

+ When and how should the customers be informed about the change?

+ What are the customers' expectations likely to be, and how can those expectations be managed?

Step 8. *Sustain Engaged Team Performance*

One of the metrics that the department decided to formally track in the future was the cross-training status. Knowing that the ability to share work was critical to team performance, the GPS team created a matrix for the individual teams so that each team could keep track of which team members were trained on which office preferences. The matrix was placed on the whiteboard with the other metrics. The teams also set a standard for refresher training, forcing cross-trained team members to occasionally pull some quotes from each of the field offices that they could support, so that they didn't lose their capability.

The teams' assigned office lists were organized by region and by "complexity": there were two teams of "high-complexity" offices, two teams with "lower-complexity" offices, and two teams that covered offices that needed a slightly different process for doing quotes. This reorganization of the teams enabled a different development path, where new team members would be onboarded to the two low-complexity teams and more experienced associates could move up to a higher-complexity team as their product knowledge grew.

Whole books have been written on skills assessment and job design, and we won't repeat that content here. Candidly, we often find that some of those books can encourage people to overthink the roles, skills assessment, and job design before they challenge the process, metrics, and norms. But obviously we agree that once you decide what's important to know and do, the leadership team needs to provide appropriate opportunities for associates to develop, *track*, and sustain the requisite skills and knowledge.

Leading Engaged Team Performance is different.

In 2008, we had the great fortune to bring another team that was starting a new performance transformation project on a tour of the GPS area. Coincidentally, one of the former leaders of the new project's department had recently been transferred to GPS and was our tour guide. So, all the leaders in the new project's department knew her and trusted her, and she knew the challenges that they faced because she used to work with all of them. After hearing her enthusiastic description of the process and the metrics during the tour, one of them asked her a great question: "So, what's different about your job now?"

Initially, she scared them by saying, "Well, you might think this is a bad thing, but I spend a half hour every morning to make sure the metrics are posted and the team sees them. We have a team huddle to discuss the current status, yesterday's performance, and any special situations."

Heads nodded. One person commented, "Yeah, we'd never have the extra time to do that data work." Just for a moment, I was worried.

But then the tour guide–leader said, "And after that, I don't have to do anything special to make sure the work gets done. I don't have to check to make sure people are working. I don't have to move resources around. I don't have to babysit anything or anybody. The team takes care of the work. You know me, and I know what you have to deal with in your department, because

I used to work with you. The difference is that I spend a half hour on the metrics and then I get to be proactive all day. I get to spend the day doing my job, interacting with our customers, and developing people." Wow!

After leading the transition, leaders need to provide the ongoing coaching to sustain the team's skills, monitor the work, and continue to improve both process and performance. The leader's job in an ETP team becomes a lot more fun.

Discussion Questions

+ Would you rather lead an engaged team that thinks for itself, or would you rather lead a group of individuals, with individual goals, who do precisely what you tell them to do?

+ Will Engaged Team Performance work if you only do some of the steps? For example, can you implement the performance steps without first studying the process?

+ What advice would you give to a new supervisor or manager joining this area?

Resources

This case study is available for training and education purposes. For more information, please contact us at:

www.engagedteamperformance.com

or

www.implementationpartners.com/engaged_team_performance.html

Or feel free to drop us an e-mail at:

info@implementationpartners.com

All the best!
Dodd Starbird and Roland Cavanagh

Bibliography

Belasco, James A., and Ralph C. Stayer, *Flight of the Buffalo: Soaring to Excellence, Learning to Let Employees Lead*, New York: Warner Books, 1993.

Brafman, Ori, and Rod A. Beckstrom. *The Starfish and the Spider: The Unstoppable Power of Leaderless Organizations*, New York: Penguin Group, 2006.

Drucker, Peter F., *Management: Tasks, Responsibilities, Practices*, New York: HarperCollins, 1974.

————, *Managing in the Next Society*, New York: St. Martin's Press, 2002.

Elliott, Ord, *The Future Is Fluid Form*, New York: iUniverse, 2009.

Goldratt, Eliyahu M., and Jeff Cox, *The Goal*, Great Barrington, MA: North River Press, 1984.

Hackman, J. Richard, *Leading Teams*, Boston: Harvard Business School Publishing Corporation, 2002.

Hammer, Michael, and James Champy, *Reengineering the Corporation: A Manifesto For Business Revolution*, New York: Harper-Collins, 2001.

Kaplan, Robert S., and David P. Norton, *The Balanced Scorecard: Translating Strategy Into Action*, Boston: The President and Fellows of Harvard College, 1996.

Katzenbach, Jon R., and Douglas K. Smith, *The Wisdom of Teams*, Boston: Harvard Business School Press, 1993.

Marston, Cam, *Motivating the "What's in It for Me" Workforce: Manage Across the Generational Divide and Increase Profits,* Hoboken, NJ: John Wiley & Sons, 2007.

Merholz, Peter, Todd Wilkens, Brendon Schauer, and David Verba, *Subject to Change: Creating Great Products and Services for an Uncertain World,* Sebastopol: CA, O'Reilly Media, Inc., 2008.

Miller, Eric, *Socio-Technical Systems in Weaving, 1953-1970: A Follow–up Study,* Human Relations.1975; 28: 349-386

Pande, Peter, Robert Neuman, and Roland Cavanagh, *The Six Sigma Way: How GE, Motorola, and Other Top Companies Are Honing Their Performance,* New York: McGraw-Hill, 2000.

———, *The Six Sigma Way Team Fieldbook: An Implementation Guide for Process Improvement Teams,* New York: McGraw-Hill, 2002.

Pasmore, William, *Action Research in the Workplace: A Sociotechnical Perspective,* reprinted, London: SAGE Publications, 2001.

Rother, Mike, and John Shook, *Learning to See,* Brookline, MA: The Lean Enterprise Institute, 1999.

Stack, Jack, with Bo Burlington, *The Great Game of Business,* New York: Doubleday, 1992.

Tapscott, Don, *Growing Up Digital—The Rise of the Net Generation,* New York: McGraw-Hill, 1998.

Tapscott, Don, and Anthony D. Williams, *Wikinomics: How Mass Collaboration Changes Everything,* New York: Portfolio, a member of Penguin Group (USA) Inc., 2008.

Taylor, Frederick W., *The Principles of Scientific Management,* New York and London: Harper & Brothers Publishers, 1911.

Trist, E., G. Higgin, H. Murray, and A. Pollock, *Organizational Choice: Capabilities of Groups at the Coal Face under Changing Technologies: The Loss, Re-discovery and Transformation of a Work Tradition,* London: Tavistock, 1963.

Tulgan, Bruce, *Not Everyone Gets a Trophy: How to Manage Generation Y*. San Francisco: Jossey-Bass, 2009.

Wheeler, Donald J., *Understanding Variation: The Key to Managing Chaos*, Knoxville, TN: SPC Press, 1993.

Womack, James P., and Daniel T. Jones, *Lean Thinking*, New York: Simon & Schuster, 1996.

Womack, James P., Daniel T. Jones, Daniel Roos, and Donna Sammons Carpenter, *The Machine That Changed the World*, New York: HarperCollins, 1990.

Index

About the Authors

Implementation Partners

Dodd Starbird and Roland Cavanagh are the managing partners and coowners of Implementation Partners LLC, a consulting company that delivers game-changing results for clients through a collaborative focus on helping clients listen to their customers' needs, analyzing data, streamlining processes, and driving performance. The company's partners have pioneered Engaged Team Performance (ETP), an approach that drives process and performance excellence to achieve dramatic improvements in business results. Implementation Partners has delivered over $350 million in financial impact for its clients in the last two decades.

Results. Delivered.

Dodd Starbird has 20 years of global business leadership experience in consulting, strategy, sales, finance, manufacturing, systems, quality, operations, human resources, and distribution management.

Dodd began his career in 1990 with the U.S. Army, achieving the rank of captain, and in 1996 he joined Coors Brewing Company to lead two production teams and facilitate Lean process improvement efforts for its manufacturing operations. In his last role at Coors, Dodd led the warehouse and delivery operation for the company's flagship Denver distribution center. He spearheaded a number of high-profile Lean Six Sigma projects for Cordis, a Johnson &

Johnson Company, and then in 2001 he began his career as a consultant, becoming a coowner of Implementation Partners in 2004.

In his current role as a managing partner, Dodd leads change efforts that consistently achieve exceptional results for clients by integrating best-in-class process redesign, team performance, and change management tools together with broad business management, engaging leadership, and deep strategy deployment experience.

Dodd has a bachelor of science in mechanical engineering from the United States Military Academy at West Point and an MBA from the University of Denver. He lives in Atlanta, Georgia, with his wife, Celeste, and their four children, James, Aspen, Autumn, and Jade.

Roland R. Cavanagh, PE, is the author of *What Is Design for Six Sigma?* and coauthor of the popular business books *The Six Sigma Way: How GE, Motorola and Other Top Companies Are Honing Their Performance* and *The Six Sigma Way Team Fieldbook: An Implementation Guide for Process Improvement Teams*, published by McGraw-Hill.

Roland brings 34 years of leadership experience in consulting, product design, manufacturing, systems, quality, and operations to clients in industries ranging from energy, utilities, consumer products, retail, software and hardware to financial services, distribution, and medical devices, worldwide.

He has a proven ability to get results for clients by leading breakthrough change efforts using world-class tools and his expertise in planning, designing, leading, and coaching the implementation of strategic business improvement deployments.

Roland has a bachelor of science degree in mechanical engineering from the University of California, Davis, and is a Registered Professional Engineer (Mechanical). Roland and Jan Cavanagh live in Jamestown, Rhode Island, when they're not on their boat somewhere on the Eastern Seaboard or pestering their son, Barrett, who is pursuing degrees in mechanical engineering and engineering management at the University of Vermont in Burlington.